IMPRINTS O

IMPRINTS OF THE FUTURE

POLITICS AND INDIVIDUATION
IN OUR TIME

George Czuczka

With a Foreword by
Ann Belford Ulanov

DAIMON
WASHINGTON
ZÜRICH

All rights reserved. No part of this publication may be reproduced or transmitted in any form or by any means, electronic or mechanical, including photocopy, recording or any information storage and retrieval system without written permission from the publisher.

Original Cover Illustration: Joel T. Miskin

Library of Congress Cataloging-in-Publication Data

Czuczka, George T.
Imprints of the future.

Bibliography: p.
Includes index.
1. Political psychology. 2. Individualism.
3. Jung, C. G. (Carl Gustav), 1875-1961. I. Title.
JA74.5.C98 1987   320'.01'9   87-51145
ISBN 3-85630-513-0 (Switzerland)

Copyright ©1987 by Daimon Verlag
CH-8840 Einsiedeln, Switzerland

Printed in The United States of America

Contents

	Foreword	v
	Preface	ix
1.	The Keys of Paradise	1
2.	A Golden Chain	6
3.	An Almost Endangered Species	12
4.	Searching for the New Man	18
5.	A Maginot Line of the Mind	22
6.	The Oldest President Ever	27
7.	A Revolution of Nihilism	32
8.	A Course of Empire	38
9.	The Salvation Bazaar	48
10.	An Almost Chosen People	54
11.	Emancipation and Convergence	62
12.	The Anatomy of Transformation	70
13.	Thresholds and Crossings	80
14.	The Archetype of Futurity	89
15.	The Tempest Revisited	95
	Bibliography	101
	Index	109

Foreword

Fortunately we have outgrown the short-sightedness that often afflicted the infancy of depth psychology. It was a narrow vision that posited a false dichotomy between inside and outside life, between individual and society, between personal growth and political. People generally recognize now what many depth psychologists knew from the beginning, that there is no self without connection to society and no society without individual selves. C. G. Jung puts it bluntly in his description of the Self as the center of the whole psyche, conscious and unconscious: when the Self is genuinely reached, it spontaneously creates a group.

Few books address the political scene by focusing on its underlying psychodynamics, which some of us see as a major need. The author of this book meets that need and does so with particularly apt attention to the future, its perils and its possibilities. From his background in the U. S. Foreign Service, he finds hope for the world's future to lie in increased psychological vision, and makes the basis for that hope into a persuasive argument. Many may indeed have some sense of a unitary world and a participatory universe where all of us are involved and none of us can stand aside as mere observers. But we are also uncomfortably aware of a critical loss of values as typical of our times, that leaves not only nations but individuals to drift in nihilistic emptiness, What do we do against this emptiness? Materialistic solutions do not work. Attempts at a kind of totalitarian discipline may cover over but do not heal this burnt-out state, any more than addictions to food, drugs, or self-righteous moralizing. The loss of soul is too much for nations and individuals.

The link between our present anguish over social and political fragmentation and our hope for future integration, the author argues, lies in the human psyche. Separately and together, we may enlarge our conscious connection with the unconscious forces both in us and around us. There may lie the way out of our emptiness.

Using Jung's notion of the ego as the center of conscious identity, of individual and group, and the Self as the center of the psyche, the author moves persuasively into Jungian territory. First, we are reminded that the Self is set in motion precisely at times of impasse when traditional values seem to have lost their vitality and relevance. Then and there, in that darkness hope is born. Second, we must remember that our projection onto others of psychic attitudes and contents which really belong to ourselves is more than just a cause of strife; it also reflects our unconscious desire to know more about our enemy and ourselves. I should add that since projection is one of the ways we become conscious of what really belongs to us, it is also one of the ways we involve ourselves with others. Becoming conscious of self means increased consciousness of others; self-interest becomes social concern. Finally, the author wisely reiterates the important distinction between individualism and Jung's notion of individuation. Individualism, as usually pursued, looks to satisfy the ego's ambitions, whether the satisfactions are biological, material, or political. In individuation, becoming an individual and indivisible self occurs only with consciousness of our kinship with others.

Individuation brings consciousness of our major community of interests with others, where we share the same kind of unconscious life. The paradoxical textures of that mixing of consciousness and the unconscious give George Czuczka's book its animating strength and conviction.

Ann Belford Ulanov
Professor of Psychiatry and Religion
Union Theological Seminary

New York City, March 1987

Preface

Imprints of the Future seeks to demonstrate the relevance of Jungian psychology to the political process and to international relations. The book, which spans a period of 500 years—roughly from the discovery of America to the rise of Reagan, Gorbachev, and the Ayatollah—explores the fate of political dreams and the reality of political actions.

The *imprints* of the title correspond to the archetypal data "which from time immemorial have determined the psychic structure as it now exists"[1] and which have been and will continue to be our "companions on the road of life," [2] as Jung says. In that sense, they are binary, Janus-like, allowing us to experience multiple dimensions of time, as if in a dream; granting us a kind of panoptic vision of the past and future.

The specific premise of the present book is that the Jungian approach is not restricted to the analytic encounter or even to the solitary individual but that it can contribute to healing the split and bridging the gap which separates nations, ideologies and religions.

Jung's unique Swiss vantage point, in the eye of the hurricane of two world wars, enabled him to observe the catastrophic and cataclysmic events in the surrounding world and led him to conclude that modern man stands at the threshold of a new spiritual epoch. There is a "longing for rest in an age of unrest," he wrote, "a longing for security in an age of insecurity." [3]

These sentiments, expressed almost sixty years ago, are as valid today as they were then. We are still waiting at the threshold and still hoping for rest and security; for a new form of existence.

Even as the big powers continue to hold their fire and ultimate war, thankfully, has been averted, the uncertainties keep on multiplying and our apprehensions are growing along with them. Once again, we are living through times that try men's souls and once again, we are searching for an anchor, a safe haven, for a hero who might take us there.

We may be desperate; we may be defiant—but above all we are vulnerable, eager to grasp at straws, discovering saviors where there are none; transforming cardboard figures into heroes; looking to admirals, colonels and holy ghost entertainers for spiritual guidance and moral leadership; continually asking questions which seem, if anything, to compound the very ambiguities they attempt to reconcile.

Why is it, we ask, that as powerful a nation as the United States, though armed to the teeth, still lives in almost constant fear of annihilation? How can America be standing tall even as it is being cut down to size? How can we remain masters of our own house even as the spirit no longer truly moves us? What good does it do to be shielded against all attacks by land, sea and air and from outer space, if our economy goes bankrupt in the process? And—what kind of a people are we (or have we become) that we should persuade ourselves to embrace those who openly deceive us?

Obviously, no single book—however well-intentioned and researched—can provide definitive answers to any or all of these questions or lay down a foolproof program of action to get us from here to there. At best, it can draw comparisons, point out analogies, jog our collective memory and outline something of an agenda for the individual to follow as he or she tries to make an impact on the collective by bringing about change within himself.

Jung's own position in this regard is clear. "In the last analysis," he wrote, "the essential thing is the life of the individual. This alone makes history, here alone do the great transformations first take place, and the whole future, the history of the world, ultimately spring as a gigantic summation from these hidden sources in individuals. In our most private and subjective lives we are not only the passive witnesses of our age, and its sufferers, but also its makers. We make our own epoch."[4]

Imprints opens with a statement of principles in the form of a prologue which introduces the reader to an anxious dreamer of our own century confronted with an enigmatic promise of paradise, and a Renaissance visionary known to his contemporaries as the "Prince of Concord."

The five explicitly political chapters which follow attempt to show how the Utopian master plans of the Renaissance have come to be exploited and distorted by the savage fundamentalists of our time—culminating in Hitlerism, a collective evil which has cast such a somber shadow over this century.

The psychological damage caused by the exposure to this traumatic phenomenon continues to affect us all—in the form of racism, emptiness of soul and the temptation to turn to totalitarian prescriptions "whenever it seems impossible to alleviate political, social and economic misery in a manner worthy of man,"[5] as Hannah Arendt has said.

The next section deals with matters closer to home: with the American Dream, its ups and downs and future prospects; with America's rise to big power status by virtue of its wealth, abundance and nuclear arsenal—which has not been accompanied by a gain in the kind of inner strength needed to resolve the great moral conundrums of the present and the future. Big power status, it is suggested, only serves to magnify a nation's moral responsibilities while diminishing its range of choices and freedom of action. For America and the other big powers, the choices are narrow indeed— limited by the imperative need of tomorrow's unitary world for transcendence and liberation from opposites; from ethnic, racial and ideological sterotypes; from inner resistance to change, convergence and reconciliation.

The focus of the fourth major segment of the book is on the Jungian concept of individuation and the role it might play in bringing about significant social and political change. Jung himself addressed the broader implications of the individuation process, describing it as "the full flowering not only of the single individual, but of the group, in which each adds his portion to the whole."[6] This is the challenge to which Western men and women might rise and perhaps the most useful and enduring contribution they can make to peace, integration and solidarity among the various parts of the globe—regaining their own faith and self-esteem in the bargain.

The book ends with a brief epilogue which closes the circle, taking us back to the Renaissance; to Shakespeare's *Tempest* and the enchanted island which is America; to Prospero, the lone magician and discoverer, who undergoes a liberating experience of his own by passing through that narrow door where "the soul of everything living begins;

where I am indivisibly this *and* that," as Jung has said; "where I experience the other in myself and the other-than-myself experiences me."[7]

REFERENCES

1. C. G. Jung, *The Type Problem in Poetry* in Collected Works, vol. vi. (Princeton, NJ: Princeton University Press, 1971), p. 169.
2. Ibid., p. 170.
3. C. G. Jung, *The Spiritual Problem of Modern Man* in Collected Works, vol. x. (Princeton, NJ: Princeton University Press, 1970), pp. 91-92
4. C. G. Jung, *The Meaning of Psychology for Modern Man*. Ibid., p. 149.
5. Hannah Arendt, *The Origins of Totalitarianism*. (Cleveland and New York: World Publishing Co., 1958), p. 459.
6. C. G. Jung, *The Mana Personality* in Collected Works, vol. vii. (New York: Pantheon Books, 1953), p. 238.
7. C. G. Jung, *Archetypes of the Collective Unconscious* in Collected Works, vol. xi, part 1. (Princeton, NJ: Princeton University Press, 1969), pp. 21-22

1
The Keys of Paradise

> *Man has always been trying to understand and to control his environment, but in the early stages this process was unconscious. The matters which are problems for us existed latent in the primitive brain; there, undefined, lay both problem and answer; through many ages of savagery, first one and then another partial answer emerged into consciousness; at the end of the series, hardly completed today, there will be a new synthesis in which riddle and answer are one.[1]*

Let us begin with a dream cited by C. G. Jung in a number of his writings over a period of more than thirty years. It is a so-called "big dream"—one which reaches out beyond the dreamer's limited and personal world and speaks to him and through him with the ambiguous and oracular eloquence of powers far greater than he.

This dream, the gist of which is quickly told, was neither one of Jung's own, nor a dream of one of his patients. It was the dream of a young theology student whom Jung had never met.

In his dream, the student is the pupil of the "white magician," a venerable old man dressed entirely in black. Before long, they are joined by the "black magician," dressed entirely in white, who has just returned from a quest in a faraway country in the course of which he found the keys of paradise. But since he does not know how to use them, he has come to the white magician for help. At this crucial moment, however, the dream breaks off and the student awakens.[2]

Jung himself was primarily concerned with the dream's religious connotations and its affinities with Eastern systems of belief, as embodied in the conjunction of opposites.[3] But it may be equally appropriate to let the dream speak for itself in its own historical context—the unsettled climate of the Nineteen Twenties, an age of discontinuity oscillating between the extremes.

The student's wavering attitude might then be seen as a reflection of the predicaments of the outer world and the paradise symbol would not just refer to the Biblical garden of innocent delights but more tangibly perhaps to visionary political landscapes being invoked at the time.

If the situation as the student experienced it then was polarized, it surely is even more polarized today. The puzzles and incongruities have continued to multiply and the conflicts of interest on all levels have become ever more acute and intractable. And as for magicians, we have had more than our share of them in this century.

They have come in all shapes, sizes and guises, masquerading as philosophers, men of science, holy men or, simply, men of the people animating and galvanizing the longings for another, better world—the American Dream, the Third Rome (sacred or secular) of the Russians, the Third Reich of the Germans, the promised land wherever and whatever it might be—or playing on man's deep-seated fears of losing paradise forever.

Even those not directly affected by firestorms, concentration camps, one-party states and one-dimensional ideologies have been scarred by these nearby and faraway events and experiences and may, in that sense, be considered victims as well: exposed, like the dreamer, to the unrelenting pressure of opposites; pinned down in a no man's land between Paradise and Armageddon, the two outer limits of time.

In the so-called primitive societies, the shaman, magus or medicine man is or was assigned the task of reestablishing communication between Earth and Heaven and affording ordinary mortals a glimpse of paradise. This serves the dual purpose of satisfying the sacred and profane (or political) needs of the community, preserving its inner stability and self-esteem and assuring its spiritual continuity and psychological survival.

The great religions of the world tell of a paradisic state in the beginning and again in the hereafter. Myths, legends and fairy tales also speak of a better world which existed once upon a time. Even the political religions of our age—fascism, Hitlerism, Stalinism, to name but a few—hold out the promise of a better world in the future. But no matter how paradise is defined: as an ideal place or ideal condition, a life free from fear and want now and forever, not even magic, as the student discovers, can bring it about.

His dream ends equivocally and without issue, presumably mirroring his personal situation. He remains ensnared by the magicians' spell, appearing as a dwarf in his own dream, casting himself in a subordinate role, a walk-on part, as if unfit to perform any other, hoping against hope that they will bring order to his world. And yet, all the while, he remains unsure of their precise identities; unable to decide which of the two to trust and whether to turn to the right or left.

In the end, the keys of paradise, for all their mantic power, do not fit in either world. The gates of paradise do not fly open; the light of the world does not shine forth. Paradise itself, whatever the dreamer understands by it, remains unattainable. The way out of the existential maze remains barred and he himself (like so many of us today) remains rooted to the spot, trapped in an agonizing and outwardly insoluble situation.

The student, to be sure, concerns us only as the prototype of the Western nonbeliever, who searches but cannot find; who is forced to choose but cannot decide. His passivity concerns us because it is symptomatic of the moral dilemma which continues to confront us. His neurosis concerns us because we know it to be our own.

In this specific sense, the student's dream was indeed a "big" dream because it encapsulated the human condition of an entire age: the sense of hesitation; the fear of crossing the threshold; the fear of what lies beyond and, at the same time, the tantalizing vision of a different, freer state—free of the gross anxieties, brutalities and famines with which we now live.

We might wish—for the student's sake as well as our own—that the dream had turned out differently: bright with promise, pointing to a better future by its example, providing evidence of a healing trend within individuals and, through them, the world-at-large.

The dream we have in hand holds out no such hope. But we who have inherited the student's conundrum must keep on trying to resolve and respond to it and determine as best we can whether, how and when the keys of paradise might fit. This errand, which we cannot in good conscience ignore, is at the heart of this book.

REFERENCES

1. Alfred Ernest Crawley, *The Idea of the Soul*. (London: A. & C. Black, 1909), p. 11.

2. C. G. Jung, *Archetypes of the Collective Unconscious* in Collected Works, vol. ix, part 1. (Princeton, NJ: Princeton University Press, 1969), p. 34.

3. Ibid., p. 36.

2
A Golden Chain

> *These were the years...when the decision was taken to honour the Christian, pagan and humanist divinities in three ideologically united sanctuaries...The three temples are so intimately linked that the scheme for their construction must have been conceived as a whole.*[1]

The dream of paradise brings back the memory of the original state of unity "in which the contraries exist side by side without conflict,"[2] as the religious historian Mircea Eliade has said, and gives rise to the desire to restore that harmony. It is a recurrent dream that is most likely to emerge as an inner response to outer upheaval and transistion—representative of that peculiar blend of impatience and nostalgia; that eagerness to move on and unwillingness to let go of the past which often marks the breach between two time frames.

One such psychological moment occurred in the Renaissance, five hundred years ago. The old culture was waning; traditional systems of belief had lost their vitality and validity, giving way to an age every bit as revolutionary as the present one: in cosmology, in communications, in the conduct of warfare, in unparalleled voyages of discovery.

The awakening did not take place all at once. The shift in emphasis and mood had been long in the making; gradual and cautious, mindful of the stubborn canonic and doctrinal opposition to it—perceptible primarily to the few who were responsible for bringing it about; all but imperceptible to the masses of the people who continued to live their lives in a timeless and, as it were, vertical environment, guided by the eternal verities from on high.

The future belonged to a new and impatient generation of philosophers, scientists and artists, global in outlook, rebellious in spirit; eager to catapult man into a new dimension, to reinterpret his role in the world, to formulate a new myth, to set new priorities and a new agenda.

Nowhere was the spirit of the Renaissance more vigorous and resonant than in Florence during the course of the 15th century and nowhere did the new perspective come into sharper focus than in Giovanni Pico della Mirandola's *Oration on the Dignity of Man*.

"I have placed you at the center of the world," Pico's God is saying to Pico's Adam, "so that you may more easily look around you and see everything that is in it. I created you as a being neither heavenly nor earthly, neither mortal nor immortal, so that you may freely make and master yourself, and take on any form you choose for yourself. You can degenerate into animality or be reborn towards divinity."[3]

The locale of the imaginary colloquy was a Renaissance version of the Garden, an Arcadian somewhere—no doubt on the sixth day—when God created and presumably emancipated man, bestowing upon him the inalienable right to shape his own destiny. In this sense, the *Oration* marked a great divide: it conceived of a new species of human being, capable of self-transformation, forever confronted with the moral alternative of aspiring to higher consciousness or succumbing to a lifetime of unknowing. The paradise episode, to all intents and purposes, was a rite of passage—signaling the birth of humanism or secular humanism, as some would say.

In his introduction to a collection of Pico's writings, Paul Miller recalls that Pico spoke of himself as an explorer. "His explorations extended over the whole of philosophy, but were directed by a definite purpose: the discovery of the unity of truth in a harmonious and religious order...The convergence of all thought and experience, the agreement of philosophies, were, Pico believed, facts of history, but their unity was not merely empirical; Pico understood all aspects of thought and being as disclosing a common truth because they all proceeded from a common source."[4]

To picture this unbroken continuum in their mind, the Renaissance humanists returned to the ancient Homeric image of the Golden Chain,[5] symbolizing the enduring spirit of all recorded history which links one age to the next—a lifeline nourished by memory and the common experience of the sacred and the profane, to be guarded by each generation and passed on to the one succeeding it.

The *Oration* was an ecumenical manifesto, drawing on the spiritual heritage which had sustained man throughout the Christian era and on the accumulated wisdom of classical antiquity—uniting the essence of pagan religion and Church dogma, bridging the gap between Eastern mysticism and Western theology, embracing the scriptures and arcane teachings of many peoples and civilizations; wearing the masks of God which are many.

Pico's method of creating this unity out of diversity was based on "a kind of intellectual alchemy,"[6] Ernst Cassirer, the eminent Renaissance historian has said; on a careful and sharp distinction between black and white magic; on his own particular conception of the power of man as magus to make the world whole.

"Genuine magic is no art of sorcery that makes use of the aid of demonic powers. It proceeds rather from the understanding of the immanent vital interconnections of nature, from the knowledge of all the relationships and sympathies that govern her parts. The 'true' magician is he who knows the forces of nature and understands how to direct them to their proper ends, by uniting what is separate and bringing them to a common operation."[7]

Perhaps the principal reason why such a glow (and afterglow) issues from the Renaissance is this specific vision, the pursuit of this ideal, the enduring quest for harmony—the stamp impressed upon the universe by the Creator. In such a universe, man's role is to facilitate the interaction of opposites; to participate in this process himself and thereby to help fashion a third element which transcends the original two and establishes a new plateau of consciousness. The true meaning of man's existence then can only be to preserve balance; to resolve conflict; to partake in and contribute to the sympathy of all things. Living in a bifurcated world as we do, this above all appeals to our sensibilities and longings. Without romanticizing either the period or those who endowed it with its luster, it was a point of supreme synthesis—fleeting, but full of substance and potential.

And yet, when Pico died in 1494, at the age of only 31, the Renaissance had virtually run its course. The Humanist dream of unity, of Florence as the radial axis of a new golden age, had not materialized; the alchemical prospect (in Jung's words) of accomplishing "the rescue of the human soul and the salvation of the cosmos"[8] remained unfulfilled.

The Humanists had been unable to keep the Golden Chain intact: magic, trying to internalize nature, and science conquering it in open combat went their different ways. Science forged ahead on the main road of progress; magic seemingly lost its way along back streets and blind alleys.

Pico himself, who had been hailed by his contemporaries as the "Prince of Concord," was dislodged by Machiavelli's *Prince*, the prototype of the coldblooded, efficient ruler who, in Max Lerner's words, has taught succeeding generations "to distinguish between man as he ought to be and man as he actually is—between the ideal form of institutions and the pragmatic conditions under which they operate."[9]

The past several centuries have been kinder to Machiavelli than to Pico. In a good many countries, man, once emancipated, has relapsed into a state of dependency: the prisoner of arbitrary bureaucracies; the hapless beneficiary of airtight social contracts; the victim of a variety of political wastelands which provide too little shelter and spiritual support.

Governments throughout the world invoke the dignity of man and the need to safeguard human rights, civil liberties and personal privacy on every conceivable occasion—but the truth is that the individual has long since been stripped of his true rank; that he stands alone in a crowd; a cipher.

REFERENCES

1. Pasquale Rotondi, *The Ducal Palace of Urbino*. (New York: Transatlantic Arts, 1969), p. 10.

2. Mircea Eliade, *The Two and the One*. (New York: Harper & Row, 1969), p. 122.

3. Giovanni Pico della Mirandola, *Oration on the Dignity of Man* in Ernst Cassirer, *The Individual and the Cosmos*. (Oxford: Blackwell, 1962), p.85.

4. Giovanni Pico della Mirandola, *On the Dignity of Man—On Being and the One—Heptaplus*. Introduction by Paul J. W. Miller. (Indianapolis, New York: Bobbs-Merrill, 1965), pp. xxv-xxvi.

5. Homer, *Iliad*, trans. Richard Lattimore. (Chicago: University of Chicago Press, 1951), Book viii, 18-27.

6. Ernst Cassirer, *Giovanni Pico della Mirandola, A Study in the History of Renaissance Ideas*. (Journal of the History of Ideas, vol. 3, No. 2, April 1942), p. 127.

7. Ibid., vol. 3, No. 3, June 1942, pp. 339-340.

8. William McGuire and R. F. C. Hull [eds.], *C. G. Jung Speaking* [Eliade's Interview for "Combat"]. (Princeton, NJ: Princeton University Press, 1977), p. 228.

9. Max Lerner, Introduction to Niccolò Machiavelli, *The Prince and the Discourses*. (New York: Modern Library, 1940), p. xxxii.

3
An Almost Endangered Species

> *A civilization can, indeed, advance and decline at the same time—but not forever. There is a limit toward which this ambiguous process moves; the limit is reached when an activist sect which represents the Gnostic truth organizes the civilization into an empire under its rule. Totalitarianism, defined as the existential rule of Gnostic activists, is the end form of progressive civilization.*[1]

A good deal of what we presently know about collectivism, the process which demeans the individual, and totalitarianism which stifles him utterly, is based on hindsight. Over the years, all over the world, we have watched outwardly hale political systems go under—wearing down or wearing themselves out at a snail's pace; mesmerized by the very forces intent on destroying them; failing to protect their political and social beliefs; eventually slipping into an Orwellian underworld of regimentation and doublethink.

The German scenario of the twenties and thirties is probably the most familiar of all: the traditional guardians of life, liberty, law, order and the pursuit of happiness grew old and weak and tired on the job—dimly aware of the limits of their power, unsure of their mission, all but vanquished in spirit. Their sense of self-doubt and inadequacy filtered down to the rank-and-file whose security and self-respect were subjected to massive strain and ultimately to irreparable damage. The painful disorders engendered by the waning of the old guard went a long way toward eroding the texture of the state and, in the end, the institutions designed to mitigate these very disorders and to absorb the shocks and tremors were themselves affected, buckling under the pressure.

The true-blue liberals thought (as some still do today) that collectivism or even totalitarianism was something that happened to others; an affliction from which their society was forever immune; a burden which would somehow pass them by. The Nazi rise to power proved them wrong. It showed that the process, once it has gathered sufficient momentum, takes on a life of its own and leaves the individual with virtually no place to hide.

After the Second World War, Max Picard, a German physician-philosopher, sought to prove that the German malady was endemic to Western society. It can strike anywhere, Picard said, when continuity breaks down; when reality splinters into a thousand isolated fragments; when the human spirit crumbles.

"The Hitler dictatorship was not a political necessity," he wrote. "It was a psychological and formal necessity in this world of discontinuity."[2] Nihilism and totalitarianism, he believed, are most likely to appear in tandem—almost by definition. Instead of having their individual and collective "hunger for wholeness"[3] satisfied, the Germans got the total state and, along with it, total domination of all aspects of life.

The *Fuehrer* may be dead and gone. Nazism, as practiced by him, has ended on the dust heap of history, Picard tells us. But the spiritual chaos which was responsible for its emergence and growth lives on. "As long as discontinuity prevails, there will be a persistent drive for some outward expression of the general inner discontinuity, be it in politics or any other field."[4]

Now if Picard, an obscure commentator at best, had been alone in reaching these dire conclusions, he could probably be shrugged off and his book returned to the shelf. But the unfortunate truth is that hundreds, thousands of respected voices—from one end of the political, economic, social and religious spectrum to the other—have been saying much the same thing for a good many years. The writers have called our age ugly names; the painters and sculptors have portrayed man as an abused, absurd and disjointed being; a long parade of horror films has implied that the end is near. Sartre held that there was no exit and Billy Graham preaches that the world is aflame.

The pundits and critics cannot all be wrong in pointing out these deviations and deformities. The present state of affairs, whether we care to admit it or not, is part and parcel of our Western heritage which we dare not deny or discard. It is the monkey on our back; it belongs to each and every one of us: secular humanists, religious traditionalists; liberals and reactionaries; war lovers and peace lovers; those who are still in the land and those who are not.

Weimar Germany, a mass democracy which strayed off course and sold its birthright, was the first advanced nation in modern times to become ungovernable by conventional means. The subtle system of checks and balances which regulates and stabilizes the operations of government had been thrown out of order and the economic, social and spiritual safety net came apart once and for all.

The liberal establishment, identified with the preservation of the status quo, argued itself out of existence; the far left did its utmost to bring down what was left of the republic and the non-Nazi right believed in the probity and historical necessity of a conservative revolution to restore the old order and resolve the cultural contradictions of modern industrial civilization.

In the end, once the inner core of the Weimar Republic had melted down, it was Hitler—the prototype of the desperate, peripheral man of our time—who picked up the pieces, fashioned a lumpen coalition composed of millions like him and went on to victory.

His *Lebensraum* and master race schemes may have lost most of their relevance in today's post-atomic, interdependent, multinational world. But who would deny that a great many people are still (or once again) fascinated by other hallmarks and eccentricities of Hitler's "revolution of nihilism:"[5] the messianic overtones of his arrival on the scene; the passionate evocation of patriotism, nationalism and preeminence; the political pragmatism and religious fervor of the movement—not to mention the appeal to the sadistic strain in men and women everywhere?

The Weimar analogy, to be sure, is no more than an analogy and the Hitler legacy is just a legacy. It would therefore be simple-minded or at best speculative to equate conditions then with conditions now; to go beyond pointing out certain obvious parallels: the extreme liberalism of the period and the intense backlash and response to it; the almost desperate search for a truly unifying principle.

But it would be just as rash and myopic to overlook the equally obvious parallel that middle-of-the-road political systems, in their efforts to combat pressure, terrorism and subversion from the left, tend to drift progressively farther to the right in the process, undermining the very values they originally set out to protect, paving the way for the very kind of radicalism they intrinsically abhor.

"Barely hidden beneath our apparent current contempt for authority is a hunger for authority ready to be exploited," writes Willard Gaylin, the director of the Hastings Center for the Study of Ethics. "We are ready for simplistic answers and jingoistic cures. Anyone who promises to recognize our slights, to correct our humiliations, to justify our rage, to restore our potency, to increase our self-respect, to punish those who are depriving us and to restore us to our birthright will be listened to. He will be listened to and followed."[6]

In America, this might ultimately bring a rather familiar, composite leadership figure to the fore: a rough rider, a smooth talker—a confidence man, the covert hero of American fact and fiction—capable of turning the conformist and collectivist traditions of late capitalism to his own advantage. His ideology would not be fascist, Nazi or Stalinist but rather of a homegrown post-liberal or post-conservative variety, and he would draw on his insolence and persuasive skills to market and sell the American dream on the cheap.

This is merely another way of saying that totalitarianism (by whatever name) is a many-headed beast. It has many faces and wears many masks and speaks with many tongues from many platforms, rostrums and pulpits.

Under the circumstances, it may well be germane to take yet another close look at the *Reich*, the Nazis and Hitler—from a somewhat different perspective this time—mustering the courage to face the Hitler in our selves (the shadow, in Jungian parlance); to see what makes him grow and glow in the dark and then, one day, cross the threshold and take over the reins.

REFERENCES

1. Eric Voegelin, *The New Science of Politics*. (Chicago: University of Chicago Press, 1952), p. 132.

2. Max Picard, *Hitler in Our Selves*, trans. Heinrich Hauser. (Hinsdale, IL: Regnery, 1947), p. 213.

3. Peter Gay, *Weimar Culture*. (New York: Harper & Row, 1970), p. 96.

4. Picard, op. cit., p. 224.

5. Heinrich Rauschning, *The Revolution of Nihilism*. (New York: Longmans Green, 1939).

6. Willard Gaylin, *The Rage Within*. (New York: Simon & Schuster, 1984), p. 157.

4

Searching for the New Man

It was an age of experimentation, not of fundamental discoveries; a restless, extrovert age, not given to that calm introspection which is usually associated with true greatness; an age of conflict not of synthesis; rich in talent, wanting in true genius.[1]

The great wars of our time have created total environments which never really disappear in peacetime. The individual, reduced to the role of an expendable, interchangeable part of the collective, finds it more and more difficult to adjust to a system which is less than total, less than perfect and which lays no claim to inerrancy, nor indeed believes in that concept. The fact is that both the total and the more liberal system tend to cause frustration and resentment—the one for being too coercive; the other for failing to provide clear guidelines and uncomplicated rules of behavior.

Like the forty or more years that have followed World War II, the forty years of peace before the Great War were not years of love and friendship but of mutual fear which bound over the hearts and souls of whole nations to their general staffs. Lenin called the war a "mighty accelerator of events."[2] If it accelerated anything, it was the flight away from history into an everlasting present uncoupled from the past; forever exposed to the perils of the future.

The war had done to people (on the home front and the battlefront) what wars so often do: it had degraded them morally; it had robbed them of a good portion of their human dignity and of many of their once deeply-held religious and secular beliefs.

Among the Germans, despair over the lost war gave rise to mounting suspicion that conspiratorial forces had been at work to deprive them of the victory that was rightfully theirs. This argument was made-to-order for Hitler. He, too, was convinced that cowards and traitors had banded together to stay the nation's hand.

While engaged in the frenzied and relentless propaganda crusade which would eventually bring him to power, he kept repeating that wars are fought to be won; that the Great War was no exception and that only a vast arms buildup would restore Germany's authority and standing in the world and instill respect and fear in the hearts of her numerous enemies.

The arms were built and used. In the thirties and forties, Hitler got his chance to direct the war machine on his own, unleashing the greatest and most costly conflict in history. It resulted in unspeakable loss of human life on all sides and brought about his nation's complete downfall—proving yet once more what those not obsessed with the art and science of warfare knew all along: that the age of winnable wars is past and that the textbook definitions of victory and defeat have become all but meaningless.

Whether they viewed the Great War as an initiation rite or simply served out their time in passive desperation, the common soldiers came out of it a kind of secret brotherhood unable to communicate their experiences to those who had not shared them and seeking the companionship of those who had. The community of suffering out there, beyond the confines of domesticity, was the only community they knew. Out there, they came to understand that every individual life in modern society is full of danger and loneliness and that it hangs by a slender thread.

Out there, many lost their sense of continuity; their link to the life they had led as ordinary citizens, supported by family ties, contained within the texture of society and bound by the civil code. Inept or criminally negligent politicians had turned these conscripts who form the backbone of the modern army into killers and abandoned them to their fate.

They had risked their lives for an old bitch gone in the teeth, as Ezra Pound later wrote; for a botched civilization.[3] Their inner resources had been strained far beyond the breaking point and their sense of leading an existence of their own, an existence that counted, was disrupted. Courage in the face of the enemy lapsed into callousness toward danger and indifference to personal suffering and at length gave way to all-pervasive, numbing dread.

These men had been to the outer limits of disillusionment to bring back word that war itself was nothing but a machine. They had been caught in it for four years, like Jonah inside the whale, and now realized that the war machine and the peace machine were analogous—each powered by the same labor force and directed by essentially the same board of governors.

The unsettling anxieties of the age, its incessant encounters with the ambiguous and unfathomable cast a shadow on the way people lived and felt and dreamed and fantasized. Their preoccupation—somewhat like ours today—was with the occult and supernatural; with real and imaginary calamities and disasters and the medium which captured the essence of this dark mood best—then as now—was film. The movie houses of Germany were like incubators in which the dreams and nightmares of a whole nation were hatched.

Rexamining the German films of the twenties is like reading yesterday's tea leaves and discovering, to one's regret, that the signs were plain enough, if only one had had the good sense and courage to see them. The cast of characters was assembling: mountebanks and zombies; gamblers and master criminals, folk heroes and supermen; proletarians, prostitutes and profiteers. All of them appeared in motion pictures—soon to become the real-life core of the Nazi party that would sweep to power in due course.

REFERENCES

1. Walter Laqueur, *Weimar, a Cultural History*. (London: Weidenfeld & Nicolson, 1974), p. 277.

2. V. I. Lenin, *Letters from Afar* in Collected Works, vol.xxiii. (Moscow: Progress Publishers, 1964), p. 299.

3. Ezra Pound, "Hugh Selwyn Mauberley" in *Collected Shorter Poems*. (London: Faber & Faber, 1968), p. 208.

5

A Maginot Line of the Mind

> *The twentieth century has witnessed a depressing number of occasions on which political leaders have done precisely what they said they were going to do, even though such actions contradicted common sense.*[1]

In 1925, Field Marshal Paul von Hindenburg, 77, victor of the Battle of Tannenberg in 1914 and, along with Ludendorff, joint loser of World War I, was persuaded to throw his hat (or helmet) in the ring and run for the Reich Presidency. The election was set for late April of that year. The campaign lasted just three weeks and when it was over, the Marshal had won a 48 percent plurality and thus something of a mandate.

The expectation was that Hindenburg would remove the blemish of defeat and humiliation; that he would restore national pride and serve as a rallying point for the combined forces of decency, hard work and thrift. In the popular mind, he seemed like the right man for the job. He was a disciplinarian; an authoritarian who believed in the singular greatness of the nation, in its missionary purpose and in his own obligation to serve, if called up to do so.

The Marshal's victory at the polls was an early warning sign, indicative of the German people's egregious need for a new unifying symbol to take the place of those which had been lost as a result of the Great War: the nation, the Kaiser, the Reich. Full of the restlessness, frustration and despair so characteristic of the Weimar years, the voters had turned to an old man, a faded star to take them into an uncertain future—evading at least temporarily the hard choices any people in the throes of disaster and despondency must eventually make.

Meantime, the search for new political formulas went on. The far left and the far right were saying that the individual could only exist as an integral part of the collective and the liberals said he could not exist without truly being himself. But as for those who were living their everyday lives, the men and women of there and then, they were—like those of here and now—trapped in an environment of muddled alternatives and multiple choices which could not but add to their bewilderment and disorientation.

Successive governments tried their luck with remedial programs based on austerity or on public spending, to get the economy going, to provide incentives to capital and labor to work together for the common good. There were booms and bull markets and there were busts and falling stock prices. In some fields, there were more jobs than could be filled; but in many others there was double-digit unemployment. The whole nation, except for the happy few, was on a wild roller coaster ride—and there was nothing the old Marshal could do to stop it.

In fact, the old President, too, turned out to be only human—not quite as stalwart and unimpeachable as he had appeared at the onset. In time, his vested interest as a member of the traditional Prussian elite got the better of him. At his behest, the state treasury disbursed hundreds of millions of marks in subsidies to Prussian landowners, which might more profitably have been used to fight unemployment and social deprivation.

The Marshal's payday came on the occasion of his 80th birthday (in 1927) when Junkers and industrialists pooled their resources to buy him a baronial country estate as a token of their appreciation. Although the President's own direct involvement in the affair was never proved, it quickly became known that his immediate staff and a member of his family had had a hand in it. It was not a full-blown scandal serious enough to bring down the entire structure (just yet) but it did serve to weaken its foundations still further. Hindenburg's image, at any rate was henceforth tainted and his stature noticeably diminished.[2]

When the trustworthiness of a political system continues to deteriorate, social theorist Sissela Bok has written, voters and candidates alike stand to lose. "Once elected, officials find that their warnings and their calls to common sacrifice meet with disbelief and apathy, even when cooperation is most urgently needed. Law suits and investigations multiply. And the fact that candidates are not expected to have meant what they said while campaigning . . . only reinforces the incentives for them to bend the truth the next time, thus adding further to the distrust of the voters."[3]

The traditional German politicians, at the state and national levels, in the executive and the legislature, persisted in trying to meet postwar cataclysms head-on with prewar rhetoric. They scheduled their speeches in parliament and at party rallies in time for the afternoon newpapers or, in later years, the evening news broadcasts and their public appearances for maximum exposure in the picture magazines and newsreels.

Each went his own way, shouting "follow me" to his adherents, regardless of their number and composition. Movements, counter-movements, groups and splinter groups formed and disbanded in quick succession as funds and enthusiasm ebbed and flowed. The young republic had grown old before its time. It became a gerontocracy not so much because old men were at its head but because it lost touch with its proud precepts and instead began clinging to old forms and pining for bygone certainties.

"Ruling groups can in their thinking become so intensely interest-bound to a situation that they are simply no longer able to see certain facts which would undermine their sense of domination," the German sociologist Karl Mannheim wrote in the late 1920's. "There is implicit in the word 'ideology' the insight that in certain situations the collective unconscious of certain groups obscures the real condition of society both to itself and to others and thereby stabilizes it."[4]

The members of the middle class, threading their way through this jungle of ambiguities and hammer blows, were like evicted tenants, without shelter; in search of security and ready answers. They had lost their bourgeois footing and were adrift on an ocean of menials and assorted flotsam of the great work force of what we now call the post-capitalist era. Monetary inflation, corporate mergers, vastly refined management and distribution techniques had downgraded shopkeepers, artisans and small businessmen into mere salaried employees subject to the vagaries of the marketplace and of boardroom strategy. The resulting erosion of home and family life turned youngsters into vandals, delinquents and dope addicts, who felt cheated of their birthright and due reward.

The young joined the dispossessed middle class, the disaffected veterans and what came to be called the Fifth Estate—the millions of unemployed marking time, standing in line to apply for the few jobs available or to collect their social security checks. Like other marginal groups, the young had no fixed values, no ingrained habits, no unshakable beliefs or vested interests. Since there was no room inside the system, they stayed out and waited until the call came to join the big parade.

REFERENCES

1. Jeffrey Herf, *Reactionary Modernism; Technology, Culture and Politics in Weimar and the Third Reich*. (Cambridge: Cambridge University Press, 1984), p. 235.

2. W. M. Knight-Patterson, *Germany from Defeat to Conquest*. (London: Allen & Unwin, 1945), p. 413.

3. Sissela Bok, *Lying: Moral Choice in Public and Private Life*. (New York: Pantheon, 1978), p. 175.

4. Karl Mannheim, *Ideology and Utopia*. (New York: Harcourt Brace & Co., 1954), p. 40.

6
The Oldest President Ever

> *The masses grew weary of all politicians, except those who proclaimed themselves to be something better than politicians and promised to lead the nation to a wonderland of national glory.*[1]

In 1932, as Hindenburg's first term came to an end, Hitler got ready to make his move. The Center and the moderate Left searched for but could not find a viable candidate of their own: a new man not beholden to the power brokers or the ideology of the past; a charismatic figure capable of electrifying the voters. In the end, they made do with the Marshal once again although he was now close to 85 and could not reasonably be expected to survive much longer.

In the preceding seven years as president, Hindenburg had never really managed to grow into the job. His grasp of domestic affairs remained as narrow and meager as it had been and his perception of the outside world never broadened with the passage of time. Perhaps he was already too old when he started; too set in his ways and his basic outlook; too rigid to adapt to increasingly rapid change. He lived only long enough to serve out two years of his second term, presiding over the demise of the republic he had sworn to uphold.

As in 1925, it took two ballots to produce a winner; only this time it was Hitler running against the Marshal.

Hitler did not win the big prize but made strong gains in terms of prestige and exposure, planting the seeds of his own agenda in the minds of the electorate.

The defenders of the Republic had formed a weak and unstable single-issue coalition for the sole purpose of electing Hindenburg to that second term. But since the coalition failed to generate a convincing program of action, it could not and did not survive the campaign. The individual partners continued to stand at the crossroads, mistaking immobility for steadfastness; waiting and hoping for an inspiration which never came.

Still, there were observant Germans who could make out the fault line running through their country, if not through all of Europe; Cassandras sensitive to the inner workings of the individual and collective psyche; capable of hearing the grass grow, as the German saying has it. One such was Siegfried Kracauer—architect, sociologist, newspaper editor and essayist:

"There are a great many people today who have two very important things in common although they do not know it: they lack a sense of high purpose and are encumbered by the emptiness of their existence. The hustle and bustle of everyday life makes them oblivious of this inner fact of life. At times, they may even feel free of the secret burden that oppresses them. But deep inside them, there is a great sadness...They are yearning for the reconstruction of their shattered world; for release from their marred and imperfect condition and the dawning of some superior order which will open its doors to them and let them in. The variety of the paths they are choosing is proof of the diversity of their spiritual needs."[2]

Although Kracauer succeeded in identifying both the problem and its root causes, he stopped short of calling for a return to traditional religious values, much less to the rigidities of organized religion as such. He seemed content to note the plethora of Western and Eastern cults to which "those who wait" [3] were drawn but unwilling or unable to synthesize the varieties of religious experience clamoring for attention and commitment of the masses—much as they still do today.

As for Hitler, he bridged the gulf in his own peculiar fashion, acting the part of savior and unifier with the conviction and skill of one possessed, bringing the nation into line even before he took over the reins of government.

To take the Nazis on in earnest, their opponents throughout the Weimar years would have had to trust their instincts and call on primitive faculties to which they no longer had access. It was on this level—in the deep shadows of the Weimar universe—that the magic Nazi formula was being concocted and on this level that a kind of government-in-exile existed for years before Hitler came out into the open, the high priest of a "political religion."[4]

In time, millions of Germans—exhausted by the long years of indecision and expediency; left to fend for themselves by their erstwhile political leaders—responded to the *Fuehrer's* preachings and blandishments, accepting him as the Messiah they so fervently hoped he was, overcoming their lingering doubts and the dim awareness of the dangers ahead; surrendering to the atavistic desire to be gathered up, taken in hand and led, no matter where.

Even during the final two or three years of the Weimar Republic the pundits still believed that political life would soon return to normal and that the Nazis were in fact a political party much like the others—subject to the upswings and downturns of the domestic and international economy, the confidence of their financial backers and the whims of the electorate itself.

When their share of the vote happened to rise, there was great apprehension among the moderates and liberals and when it fell, there was a feeling of great relief. Any Nazi misadventure or loss of momentum would raise hopes once more that some secret formula had been found (some kind of extra-strength repellent or wonder drug) that might stamp out the wretched lesion. But these were vain hopes; the Republic was literally on its last legs.

Essayist, novelist and sometime Communist Arthur Koestler lived and worked in Berlin throughout this time. In his memoirs, published forty years later, he wrote: "After the event, people asked themselves: How could we have been such fools as to twiddle our thumbs when the outcome was so obvious? The answer is that there were ups and downs and that it took thirty months, and that, owing to the inertia of human imagination, to most people it wasn't obvious at all."[5]

The system had continued to work, all in all. The state, the authorities, the police had continued to uphold constitutional guarantees and civil liberties, protecting life, limb and property as best they could. In fact, whenever the warring political factions observed a temporary truce and the acts of urban terrorism abated for a time, life seemed quite normal.

Later, when the Republic finally did go under; when totalitarian centralism had replaced democratic pluralism, the Weimar guardians who thought they had had their finger on the pulse of the nation could not agree on whether Hitler's rise beyond mere notoriety to absolute power had been inevitable or simply inconceivable.

REFERENCES

1. Hans Kohn, *The Mind of Germany*. (New York: Scribner, 1960), p. 318.

2. Siegfried Kracauer, *Das Ornament der Masse*, trans. by author. (Frankfurt/Main: Suhrkamp Verlag, 1977), pp. 106, 109.

3. Kracauer, op. cit., p. 106.

4. Eric Voegelin, *Die Politischen Religionen*. (Stockholm: Bermann-Fischer Verlag, 1939).

5. Arthur Koestler, *Arrow in the Blue*. (New York: MacMillan, 1970), p. 297.

7
A Revolution of Nihilism

> *The seizure of power by the National Socialist party and the dictatorial regime of Adolf Hitler demonstrates the possibilities of self-destruction of a modern society. This change, revolutionary in its consequences, happened in a nonviolent way, observing the legal provisions of a democratic constitution in an economically developed, socially tightly organized, and culturally highly diversified country.*[1]

Over the years, Hitler had always said that he would win the chancellorship by legal means or not at all. The politicians of the conservative right presented the post to him with a variety of strings attached: they were Liliputians tying down a Gulliver; circus clowns caging a tiger. At the swearing-in ceremony, the old Marshal was in full uniform; Hitler, attired in a black frock coat and carrying a top hat, swore an oath to protect the constitution and to discharge his duties "impartially and with justice to everyone."[2]

By now, decades after the fact, almost everybody knows, or ought to know, what Hitler's word of honor was worth and who the Nazis were, what they were after and what they actually did. No purpose is served by reading off the Nazi personnel roster again or the roster of their crimes; by performing still another autopsy on Hitler and his henchmen; by conducting yet another search of the house he built or even by sifting the ashes of the holocaust for one last definitive clue as to how and why.

The Nazis had managed to beat the Republic at its own game, ruthlessly exploiting the democratic freedoms of speech and assembly to subvert the constitution and terrorize the public. Hitler did come to power legally, it is true—by staging a revolution on the installment plan.

Once they took power, things moved incredibly fast. The lunatic Nazi fringe turned out to be a well-organized system that burst out of the shadows full-blown, with a vindictiveness and violence that came as a profound shock to a society accustomed to the rule of law. Most unsettling and degrading of all, however, was the complete reversal of values and roles. Those who had been freest and had actively championed more freedom for all were now at the mercy of men who were prisoners of their own manic ideology; and whatever inhibitions the new jailers might previously have had were swiftly shed as they began to exercise iron-fisted control over the nation.

The press and the intelligentsia were among the first to be blackballed and purged. The new regime's need was for positive thinkers and loyalists; not for watchdogs and faultfinders who were forever probing the nation's weak spots and failings. Like the Nazis, the liberal critics had been saying for years that the society was sick; but unlike the Nazis, they offered no ready cure because they could never agree on the exact nature and origin of the malady.

Their humanist world view of relative uncertainties and at best conditional answers placed severe limitations on the promises they felt entitled to make. By contrast, the Nazi world view of notably less complex and ambiguous expedients provided for a program of decisive action which could not but appeal to the millions who had been marking time for so long.

On the surface, the Nazi state was run—as most modern nations are—like a commercial, industrial and military conglomerate. During the twelve years it was in operation it ran very smoothly indeed, piling up economic and military successes—a veritable juggernaut of bureaucratic and technical efficiency. For Hitler, however, the state also served as the backdrop for an unending succession of media events. In fact, it seems as though Hitler and the media were made for each other.

"I saw him with my own eyes," Jung wrote of the *Fuehrer*. "He behaved in public like a man living in his own biography, in this case as the somber, demonic 'man of iron' of popular fiction, the ideal of an infantile public whose knowledge of the world is derived from the deified heroes of trashy films."[3]

In a very real sense, Hitler himself was a mass medium—putting his skills as a teacher, preacher and entertainer to full use in a total communications environment—serving as a sounding board of millions, translating their most secret appetites into a forceful program of seemingly riskless action.

He attacked "the system" much as "big government" is being attacked these days by the very politicians intent on taking control of it; he promised to put the country back to work (in the face of lingering unemployment) and to restore its erstwhile stature (in the face of declining prestige). He achieved both objectives by building up a vast military-industrial complex to protect the Western world against communism.

Long after he was in firm control of the state, he was still campaigning against the system he had toppled, doggedly reminding his audiences of the ruinous situation he had inherited and of his success in rescuing the nation by halting the drift toward moral and fiscal bankruptcy.

Again and again, he would go directly to the people, over the head of the surviving institutions, to seek support for his programs, policies and undertakings.

Today, the Hitler histrionics strike us as antiquated and overblown; but in his own day he was able to beguile the masses and, in speaking of social brotherhood, discipline and patriotic fervor, to conjure up the picture of a moral community of the elect that enthralled his listeners.

By allowing men and women throughout the land to share in his unique powers, visions and insights, he lifted their spirits and renewed their faith in his rectitude and credibility. In their eyes, he alone remained untarnished by the baser and quotidian aspects of political life even as his blindly loyal underlings continued to wage an unending dirty war against the forces of evil.

Hitler himself once said that he and the German people were brought together as if by a miracle.[4] In truth, of course, there was nothing miraculous about it at all. Modern-day leaders such as he need the lonely crowd as much as the lonely crowd needs them. They are drawn to each other by the force of their mutual emptiness and then proceed to feed and fill out at each other's expense.

The relationship, however passionate it may appear on the surface, is addictive, tainted, desperate—as the Hitler phenomenon and more recent experiences with esoteric and not-so-esoteric cults have shown; and the longer it lasts, the more difficult it becomes to break the bond linking the nonbeliever to the false prophet.

For the man and woman in the street, the real name of the Nazi game was *Gleichschaltung*—one of those composite German nouns which are not easily translated. Conformism, if it did not imply an at least vestigial element of free choice, would approximate its meaning. In the total Nazi universe, it meant being brought into line; following the leader; doing as you and your neighbor and your neighbor's neighbor are told. In time, the process assumed a life of its own, ultimately engulfing one and all; casting a spell over the nation.

Studying this phenomenon years later, William S. Allen, an American historian, came to the conclusion that "each group saw one or the other side of Nazism, but none saw it in its full hideousness. Only later did this become apparent, and even then not to everyone. The problem of Nazism was a problem of perception."[5]

Without a doubt, there was a massive failure of vision and imagination but it was also numbness, induced by fear, which held people back and kept resistance to a minimum.

"It was always a matter of waiting for some new, more obvious proof that the regime was evil," writes John Stoner, an American cleric, "of expecting some person in a position of authority to make the break first, and of hoping that right would ultimately prevail without requiring any personal sacrifice beyond the ordinary."[6]

The Germans' dreams, recorded at the time, all but reinforced this picture of paralysis, stripping away the outer protective layers of conformity and accommodation and revealing the regime's pervasive impact and its overwhelming power to abuse and isolate them; to penetrate to the very marrow of their existence and force them to capitulate.

One woman dreamed of no longer being able to speak for herself but only in unison with the group; another was singing Nazi songs she really thought despicable. One girl had the courage to tell a political joke but was careful not to include the punch line and another girl dreamed that she had inadvertently betrayed her Jewish boyfriend to the *Gestapo*. A man discovered his Alpine mountain guide to be a storm trooper and a young Gentile, taken for a Jew, ran from the police and hid—in a pile of corpses.[7]

REFERENCES

1. M. Rainer Lepsius, *From Fragmented Democracy to Government by Emergency Decree and National Socialist Takeover* in Juan J. Linz and Alfred Stepan, eds., *The Breakdown of Democratic Regimes: Europe*. (Baltimore, London: Johns Hopkins University Press, 1978), p. 34.

2. Robert Payne, *The Life and Death of Adolf Hitler*. (New York, Washington: Praeger, 1973), pp. 246-247.

3. C. G. Jung, *After the Catastrophe* in Collected Works, vol. x. (Princeton, NJ: Princeton University Press, 1970), p. 204.

4. Hamilton T. Burden, *The Nuremberg Party Rallies*. (New York: Praeger, 1967), p. 131.

5. William S. Allen, *The Nazi Seizure of Power* (The Experience of a Single German Town). (Chicago: Quadrangle Books, 1965), p. 281.

6. John Stoner, *The Moral Equivalent of Disarmament*, in Hal Wallis, ed., *Waging Peace*. (San Francisco and Sidney: Harper & Row, 1982), p. 240.

7. Charlotte Beradt, *The Third Reich of Dreams*, trans. Adriane Gottwald. (Chicago: Quadrangle Books, 1968), p. 51f.

8
A Course of Empire

I am waiting for a rebirth of wonder and I am waiting for someone to really discover America.[1]

It would be convenient and comforting to know that the hideous outburst of the Germans was an isolated case; that by going the route of nihilism in our stead, they heaped guilt on no one but themselves even while expiating all of our own once and future sins. Unfortunately, the Germans did no such thing; but they have given us a grisly object lesson of what happens to a civilized people which lets go and is drawn over the edge. Nietzsche had shown the way earlier. He was rent asunder as he had said all modern men would be, if they jettisoned their values and moorings and tried to conquer the void within by pursuing power without.[2]

By now, nihilism has become a state of mind and a state of affairs we experience every day—as a depreciation of values and moral judgments and as the release of destructive impulses all around us, without and within. The most common form of nihilism is a sensation of emptiness, of a gaping space which cries out to be filled. Some turn to food to fill it only to become obese; others to morality only to become self-righteous. Still others fill the void with drugs and become prisoners by choice and some fill it with nothing at all and so turn into hollow men and women.

Like so many diseases, nihilism is most easily recognized in others—particularly in adversaries both real and imaginary, in newcomers and interlopers, Wandering Jews of all faiths and other undesirables. It does not take much training in psychology to see through this process of transference and projection. Emptiness of the spirit is a heavy burden; to shift it to another's shoulders is a great relief. One's own emptiness—whatever its cause—tends to fill out with the logic of intolerance.

Life would be a lot simpler than it is if the bomb throwers, assassins and skyjackers, the perverts, subversives, addicts and misfits were alone in suffering from the disease; if they could be quarantined, sequestered, hidden from view or done away with altogether. Life could indeed be that simple, if the virus that causes the disease were not as ubiquitous and non-discriminatory as it is.

Of course there is a temptation to ask: What is Nietzsche to us? Or the German experience, for that matter. The Germans have sinned and are paying the price. Their country is divided by walls, electrified fences and contesting ideologies. But if we ask the question "What is Nietzsche to us?" earnestly and honestly, our answer will have to be: His world is our world—much as we hate to admit it. The lack of balance, the disarray of the society we live in, is personified in each of us—and Hitlerism, the 20th century underworld with which we are most familiar, lingers on. It tempts and taunts the unwary with its false promises of paradise and wholeness. It drags down the unsuspecting and brings out the Hitler in ourselves.

American psychologist James Hillman has even gone so far as to say that "we are living in a psychic concentration camp, in the sense that we are passively accepting the soulless world."[3]

Although this is fairly strong language, it is not easily disputed. True, we of the Western world live comfortably, even luxuriously—by comparison with the countless millions of other continents. But closer inspection soon reveals to us that our lives, for all their glitter and sparkle, are far too often tainted by venality, greed and lack of compassion; by a loss of soul that gives the lie to the gospel of contentment, sufficiency and national pride to which so many of us choose to subscribe.

Now in the modern, rational world, loss of soul usually goes by another name: one loses one's drive and ambition or simply feels burnt out; the inner structure becomes unglued. It can and does happen to the best of us, to the most sober and self-reliant—gradually or all at once. When the crucial moment comes, there is no mistaking it. Only then do we realize that the soul was there all along and that we need to retrieve it now that it is gone.

But if the soul is a symbol of life's meaning, as Hillman says;[4] of love given, received and shared, how can we expect to do without it for any length of time? The answer, of course, is that we cannot. We can no more do without soul than without a heart, our brain or our shadow. We may renounce and discard it, but the soul will return, in dreams and reveries or laid out like a corpse on a therapist's couch or called upon to rise and be born again at the command of some great electronic communicator.

The truth is, soul will out—and there is more than one avenue open to it. If it cannot find expression in a constructive way—which is to say in a way that heightens awareness, discernment and the strength to endure the pull of the opposing forces within and without us—then it will burst through in ways that may incapacitate and ultimately destroy us.

As for the native soul of America, it would serve no purpose here to ask what has become of it, where it has gone; what happened to the soul of the pilgrims, of the slaves and their masters and of the Orientals who built those big railroads and the immigrants who crossed the Atlantic in steerage. Conventional wisdom has it that all this stock has been reconstituted in the great American melting pot; that each tribe has added its singular bit of soul to the blend and that all Americans are the richer and better for it; that all the races, colors and creeds are dreaming the dream of paradise onward which first kindled the passions of the Puritans.

In his book-length study on Europe and the American moral imagination, Charles L. Sanford has written: "The most popular doctrine in the colonies was that America had been singled out, from all the nations of the earth, as the site of the Second Coming, and that the millenium of the saints, while essentially spiritual in nature, would be accompanied by a paradisiac transformation of the earth as the outward symbol of their inward state." [5]

So powerful was the image of an unblemished America that would redeem all of humanity in its newness and glory that Jonathan Edwards thought that the sun would henceforth rise in the West, "contrary to the course of this world, or the course of things in the old heavens and earth."[6] The sun of which he spoke was the Sun of Righteousness shining on the good men and women come to cultivate the soil of a new Eden.

The whole world was ripe for deliverance; past iniquities would serve as building blocks for a brighter future. Purification and millenial fervor swept the devil and his handiwork out to the deep blue sea and gave birth to the peculiarly American blend of high morality and earthy materialism—a winning combination which fueled the powerful engine that was and still is the American Dream.

Merely because it has come under fire, it would be a great mistake to discount the Dream or to deny its weight and luminous intensity. The Dream has remained a representation of the American spirit to this day and if America had a soul or has a soul, that is where a good part of it resides.

The splinter groups of Christianity had come from the four corners of Europe; the dissidents of another day, united in their desire to break free and create an environment where religion would be safe from the double menace of rationalism and materialism. The expanding frontier, the wide-open spaces provided the appropriate scenery and religion provided the roots the nomadic tribes of settlers and colonizers needed to sustain them as they pressed onward, forever searching for the promised land beyond the next stream or mountain range.

On the outermost edge of civilization—wherever it happened to be at a given time—the components of an orderly existence were hard to come by. Life was grim and lonely; atheism was a luxury one could ill afford.[7] The camp and revival meetings provided entertainment, a sense of community and emotional spirituality in an open-air, quasi-pagan setting by the riverside.

Throughout this time, America's soul was steadily on the move, powering the mighty forward thrust, conquering distances, moving mountains, harnessing rivers. But as it moved, it underwent subtle changes that only the vigilant were able to see. What they did see was a loss of soul—even if they did not call it such—a breach of the covenant upon which the grand experiment was founded. James Fenimore Cooper, for one, observed that America had nothing to fear but the enemy within[8]—by which he meant the soul gone astray.

The decisive shift took place in the 19th century when the garden of plenty was transplanted from the fields and orchards to the mill and factory towns. The Biblical dictate to subdue the earth was taken literally. Nature and much of her virgin land were ravished in the name of post-agrarian civilization. Domestic imperialism was in the ascendancy, sweeping every obstacle aside. The plan called for better times, more of everything and a steadily nobler breed; but the real world also produced slums, strikes and riotous capitalism.

In the late 1830's, Thomas Cole painted a grand tableau of five allegorical scenes depicting the course of empire from innocence to supreme power and eventual ruin.[9] The final canvas showed the barbarians laying waste to the city man had built, putting an end to civilization. The set of paintings was Cole's response to the sanctimonious positivism of his time and its false faith in linear progress and, at the same time, his way of bidding farewell to the grandeur of a vanishing America; the image of America as a garden. Like Cooper, with whom he maintained a close friendship, he could sense that there was a largely unexplored and unexplained dark side to the young republic—a limit to America's inward goodness and the growth of its outward power.

The public's very fasciniation with the grim subject matter; the demand for more showings at the art galleries and the seller's market in Cole lithographs all seemed to indicate that the artist's message was felt to be relevant or perhaps even prophetic. On the surface, of course, his work appeared to be dealing with other times and other lands. Doom, havoc, spoliation; man's downfall, the collapse of empire could not really have a bearing on things as they were. The nation was on its way, the great dream had just begun. The very openness of space presupposed an openness in time. As long as the frontier beckoned, time would never truly stop; the future would go on forever.

But then, two generations later, the frontier was no more; the West had been won. "What the Mediterranean Sea was to the Greeks," historian Frederick Jackson Turner said in 1893, "breaking the bonds of custom, offering new experiences, calling out new institutions and activities, that, and more, the ever retreating frontier has been to the United States directly, and to the nations of Europe more remotely. And now, four centuries after the discovery of America, at the end of a hundred years of life under Constitution, the frontier has gone, and with its going, has closed the first chapter of American history."[10]

After an interval of just five years—more likely than not in response to the closing of the frontier—the United States, having no major overland campaigns left to fight, went to sea, entering the world stage; projecting its frustrations and millenial expectations onto foreign shores.

When war came with Spain in 1898 over Cuba and the Philippines, it was as much as anything the result of a "restless aggressiveness, a desire to be assured that the power and vitality of the nation were not waning."[11] The man of the hour was Theodore Roosevelt; the man of action, the archetypal man on horseback, who felt that war and military preparedness served to keep industrialized and urbanized peoples from growing soft and purposeless.[12]

The war itself turned out to be a double-barreled affair: a crusade to liberate captive peoples and shoulder the white man's burden of missionary work and education and, at the same time, a somewhat less than virtuous escapade—to show the flag, to flex muscles and secure foreign markets.

"For pious and evangelical men," the historian Merle Curti writes, "it was possible to see God's will in the doctrine of the inevitability of overseas expansion...Those of a more secular frame of mind emphasized naturalistic rather than supernaturalistic elements in the doctrine of inevitable destiny—racial determinism and the imperatives of naval strategy, commercial interests and humanitarian obligations."[13]

The quick and easy victories over Spain in the Caribbean and the Far East produced the very kind of cathartic experience craved for by many who feared that America, only a little over one hundred years old at the time, was already losing its vigor and manliness. Although achieved at the expense of an enemy whose strength and ferocity had been vastly exaggerated, they seemed quite miraculous—even to the naval commander most directly responsible for them. "If I were a religious man, and I hope I am," said Commodore Dewey, the victor of Manila Bay, "I should say that the hand of God was in it."[14]

Theodore Roosevelt was but one in a long line of fire-eaters and Dewey one in a long line of God-fearing men of the sea—both presumably insensitive to the soul-searching voice of doubt. What they passed on to American posterity, among other things, is the image of a nation endowed with limitless physical strength and an inexhaustible reservoir of moral rectitude.

It is a haunting image that continues to persist despite a great deal of first-hand evidence of repeated American involvement and complicity in evil at home and abroad. In fact, the Civil War provides us with as poignant an example as any—an archetypal example, since it revolved around a struggle between brothers.

Properly understood, that experience alone might help to build a bridge to the dark side of the New World heritage which many an American chooses to neglect and discount. The United States somehow managed to fight the bloodiest of civil wars without—as a nation—experiencing the total calamity of it or the deep need of both sides not so much to rebuild central authority as to form a more perfect union.

America went to hell and back without being truly redeemed by the experience. The assassination of Lincoln, in fact, closed the window of opportunity that was available to a nation sick of blood-letting, bluster and self-righteousness.

No matter how Lincoln is viewed more than one century after the fact, the Herculean effort to hold it or bring it all together was there; the great attempt to heal the split, to lay the foundations for a liberation movement and then, in addition to all these, the authentic, consummate public sacrifice of his death which might have conveyed to a divided people a sense of unity based on a recognition of the tragic note that had been struck: a chance for initiation, for making the transition from innocence to maturity.

Again, it is of no consequence now which side one was on—north or south—or whether one considered Lincoln a modern-day tyrant or a martyr much like Jesus Christ. The heart of the matter was that violence had begotten untold violence which would not end and that all the human casualties and all the material damage were, in essence, self-inflicted and self-destructive. That was the tragic note; that was the low point which called for a new beginning; for a new birth of freedom, as Lincoln himself said.

American history, any history, demonstrates how difficult it is for warring brothers to make peace and achieve reconciliation. The guns have long been silent; the battlefields are national shrines now; but the war is still on. The house divided is divided still—against itself. The split is still there—not so much nationally as individually. The Civil War was a symptom. Healing, like charity, begins at home. The map of inner space is at last enlarged when the opposites within and without are bonded, when segregation gives way to integration.

REFERENCES

1. Lawrence Ferlinghetti, *A Coney Island of the Mind*. (Norfolk: New Directions, 1955), pp. 49-52.

2. William Barrett, *Irrational Man*. (Garden City, NY: Doubleday, 1962), p. 204.

3. James Hillman, *Inter Views*. (New York: Harper & Row, 1983), p. 137.

4. James Hillman, *Insearch: Psychology and Religion*. (Dallas: Spring, 1978), p. 42.

5. Charles L. Sanford, *The Quest for Paradise*. (Urbana, IL: University of Illinois Press, 1962), p. 82.

6. Jonathan Edwards, *The Great Awakening* [ed. by C. C. Goen]. (New Haven and London: Yale University Press, 1972), p. 357.

7. Amaury de Riencourt, *The Coming Caesars*. (New York: Capricorn Books, 1957, 1964), pp. 57-59, 140ff.

8. James Fenimore Cooper, *The Spy*. (New York and London: Appleton & Co., n.d.), p. 10.

9. Louis Legrand Noble, *The Life and Works of Thomas Cole*. (Boston: Harvard University Press, 1964), p. 129ff.

10. Frederick Jackson Turner, *The Significance of the Frontier in American History*. (New York: Henry Holt & Co., 1920), p. 38.

11. Richard Hofstadter, *The Paranoid Style in American Politics* (New York: Random House, 1967), p. 158.

12. Merle Curti, *The Growth of American Thought*. (New York: Harper & Row, 1943, 1951), p. 654.

13. Curti, op. cit., pp. 655-656.

14. Louis A. Coolidge, *An Old-Fashioned Senator: Orville H. Platt*. (New York: Putnam, 1910), p. 302.

9
The Salvation Bazaar

> *If family and community ties weaken and if psychic development becomes somewhat more nuclearized or even atomized, the influence of television and other distant sources may well become increasingly powerful, moving, as it were, into something like a vacuum. Between the individual and the national source of image-making there will be little or no local resistance. The middle ground of the psyche, until recently thick and rich and resistant, will have become attenuated.[1]*

Alexis de Tocqueville, writing in the 1830's, listed religion among the "causes which tend to maintain"[2] democracy in America—and for good reason. He had discovered that the multiplicity of sects (as he called them) made for greater tolerance and that the separation of church and state enabled the two to exist peacefully side by side and even enjoy the fruits of their marriage of convenience. He also noted that Americans were as pragmatic about religion as about most other aspects of life; that they worshiped as much from force of habit as from conviction but that the twin concepts of liberty and Christianity were embedded and intertwined in the American mind and, if anything, constituted the uniqueness of the American spirit.

The missionary zeal of New Englanders who made their way to far-off Missouri or Illinois to spread the gospel and extend the frontiers of Christianity led him to conclude that religious ardor in America was perpetually being warmed by the fires of patriotism. And even if religion occupied no official status in the affairs of government, its impact on society as a whole was formidable and pervasive.

The fires of religion and patriotism are still burning as brightly as they did in de Tocqueville's day but the dividing line between church and state is not as easily defined as it was then. There is, in fact, a growing disposition on the part of the clergy to cross it, and an eagerness to give priority to technique at the expense of substance. Although this may already have been true when preachers and their flocks gathered at the riverside, it is even truer now that they have gone electronic.

Clearly, it was just a matter of time before religion would turn to television to carry its message to today's far-flung converts. Some of the more enthusiastic performers have in fact developed and perfected a veritable "technology of salvation"[3] that is surely more than once removed from the authentic meaning of ministry. And though they profess to deplore the prevailing secular climate, they do not disdain to use the vacuous, fashionable vocabulary of science and rationalism to tell their story and the machinery science and rationalism have devised to help them spread it.

In many instances, the message is quasi-devotional—researched, processed and marketed with the same care and skill as any other prime-time offering. It is an assertive and unvarnished message, specifically tailored to the perceptions and needs of secular men and women without a God to call their own; an electronic catechism which says that the Bible is inerrant; that the Gospel is to be taken as the gospel truth; that positive thinking will create wealth and physical wellbing; that negative thinking, which brings the opposite, is a sin and that the poor are poor for the simple reason that they do no work hard enough.

As distinct from liberation theology, which aims to combine the political and spiritual emancipation of the exploited masses, this homegrown American variant not only supports the present political, economic and social system but exalts and defends it against all comers, viewing God as one more (albeit supremely valuable) commodity in a consumer society—a God, as religious author Richard Quebedeaux has said, who "exists because he is useful, and...helps those who help themselves."[4]

The work of salvation, the colossal task of redemption, the audience is told, has already been accomplished; the supreme sacrifice on the Cross was a grand one-time event that has a bearing on our present situation only insofar as it lifts the heavy burden off our shoulders and cleanses us of all our sins. In this way, we are saved—as if by magic—in the flickering privacy and semi-darkness of our own living room.

This formula succeeds—at least for a time—because it is a functional response to, and compensation for, the vast empty spaces of contemporary life which remain unfilled despite all the goods, services and entertainments available to us. Without a doubt, the secular temple which has been built in lieu of the one dedicated to the old God of the Mideast, of Rome and Wittenberg is a cold and lonely place. It provides a convenient location for celebrating tangible and temporal achievements—but fails to satisfy our innermost needs. What our lost soul really craves for is to be addressed directly and to get straightforward answers to increasingly complex questions—from just about anyone who offers to explain what has become hopelessly tangled and contradictory.

But just as the studio and home audience cannot be characterized as a congregation in the strict sense of the word, the electronic preachers themselves do not qualify as genuine spiritual leaders.

In fact, says Quebedeaux, it really does not matter whether they "personally believe or practice what they preach and teach over radio and TV, any more than it matters whether the actors in an 'inspiring' movie actually believe or practice in daily life the lines they are saying."[5]

Essentially, the preachers are political activists, fanning the flames of patriotism and religion yet once more in a bid to create a viable, if nostalgically tinged, us-and-them ideology for our time—in tune with a mass audience accustomed to image-builders and instant celebrities and conditioned to an unremitting flow of flat imagery and shallow information which tells no real tales and provides no real nourishment for the soul.

Thus far, no one of the television clerics has emerged as an authentic spokesman for all the rest and as a plausible leadership figure for the nation as a whole. Though they are all perpetually making incursions into the political arena on the local, state and national level, their efforts are by and large uncoordinated; punctuated intermittently by internecine warfare. For the present, it is still every man for himself, fighting his own battles in the rating wars and fund-raising sweepstakes.

The needs of secular constituencies, church congregations and the footloose electorate being at bottom much the same, however, such a leader might, in a figurative sense, be invented—or discovered, like a "found object." He and his followers would then proceed to use each other in the way the Dadaists and Surrealists used the debris and litter they found in the wastebins of everyday life to produce their canvases.

Out of the bits and pieces of some such individual, searching for his own soul, trying to find himself, they might fashion a latter-day savior, and out of the ragged assortment of their bitter feelings and anxieties, the leader himself would paste and patch together a crazyquilt political movement.

He might prove to be a preacher, a politician, a great manipulator—substituting style for substance, pledged to "apple-pie authoritarianism," in the words of political analyst Kevin Phillips, "a communications-based, high-technology, corporate-linked, frequently plebiscitary, intermittently populist conservatism. The morality of the majority would be upheld and enforced, though with politically convenient lapses. 'The Star-Spangled Banner' would wave with greater frequency and over many more parades; increased surveillance would crack down on urban outbreaks and extreme political dissidents."[6]

Is this a credible scenario for a nation as pluralistic as the United States? An island continent of the blessed and elect; Fortress America masquerading as the city on the hill; a (white) ghetto walled off against the forces of social change and oblivious to the domestic and worldwide trend toward religious, political and economic liberation: Which version of the Promised Land will it be?

Both the right and the left feel that present practices and techniques are inadequate and inappropriate to the exigencies and threats of the future: the right being mesmerized by the division of the world into two camps; the left being animated by the syncretistic vision of a global community. Both sides, in fact, are fond of speaking of the need for, or the imminence of, a new awakening. In the eyes of some authorities on the subject, such as Brown University's William McLoughlin, America is already in the midst of one.

"The reason an awakening takes a generation or more to work itself out is that it must grow with the young; it must escape the enculturation of the old ways. It is not worthwhile to ask who the prophet of this awakening is or to search for new ideological blueprints in the works of the learned. Revitalization is growing up around us in our children, who are both more innocent and more knowing than their parents and grandparents. It is their world that has yet to be reborn."[7]

REFERENCES

1. Michael Novak, *Television Shapes the Soul* in Douglas Cater and Richard Adler, eds., *Television as a Social Force*. (New York: Praeger, 1975), p. 13.

2. Alexis de Tocqueville, *Democracy in America*, vol. I, Ch. xvii. (New York: Knopf, 1953), p. 288f.

3. Richard Quebedeaux, *By What Authority: The Rise of Personality Cults in American Christianity*. (San Francisco: Harper & Row, 1982), p. 77.

4. Quebedeaux, op. cit., p. 89.

5. Quebedeaux, op. cit., p. 154.

6. Kevin P. Phillips, *Post-Conservative America: People, Politics, and Ideology in a Time of Crisis*. (New York: Random House, 1982), p. 239.

7. William G. McLoughlin, *Revivals, Awakenings and Reform*. (Chicago and London: University of Chicago Press, 1978), p. 216.

10
An Almost Chosen People

We have come full circle. Our human situation no longer permits us to make armed dichotomies between those who are good and those who are evil, those who are right and those who are wrong. The first blow dealt to the enemy's children will sign the death warrant of our own.[1]

The explosion of the first atomic bombs, followed by public recognition of their devastating potential, and man's forays beyond the pull of gravity have signaled a new psychological climate and created a new set of apocalyptic images. This, in turn, has permitted a sizable scientific-mythological complex to emerge which engages in the mass production of contemporary sagas and legends of redemption and deliverance or of retribution and the ultimate Twilight of the Gods; of unexplained flying objects and visitations from outer space.

When Jung turned his attention to this latter phenomenon during the final years of his life, he did not do so on a whim or because senility was at last overtaking him, but because he realized that the world was witnessing the birth pains of a new myth emerging from the depths of the unconscious.

"Physical hunger needs a real meal and spiritual hunger needs a numinous content," he wrote in commenting on a patient's dream about 'interplanetary machines.' "Such contents are by nature archetypal and have always expressed themselves in the form of natural revelations."[2]

Our ancestors were convinced that any signs which appeared in the heavens came from God and we, too, seem to believe that the odd little men and the sages in their flowing robes disembarking from their vehicles are bearing a message for us. The pessimists among us see the space travellers as angels of darkness; as monsters and man-eaters intent on doing us in. The optimists on the other hand, view the aliens as good shepherds or rescuers who would carry us away with them or at least perform a kind of cosmic bailout which will clean up the ecological, spiritual and psychological mess we have made of the planet.

On the screen, between the covers of a book, in our imagination and our dreams, they keep coming because something inside us keeps calling out to them; and those vehicles in which they travel all are round and luminous—symbols of the wholeness, as Jung has said,[3] we so desire even while it continues to elude us.

The extraterrestrials descending upon us come in various shapes, sizes and guises: some are humanoid, some are not; some are benign and enlightened, far above us in mind and spirit and some are caricatures of ourselves, reflections of the shadow world of our prehistoric and most recent barbaric past. All these projections of our innermost fears and longings must be contended with: they will go with us into the next age; they will hound us and continue to taunt us unless we find ways of coming to terms with them.

As for a better future (in the shape of utopia on earth or the keys of paradise), it will have to be earned rather than simply doled out to us by the Lord of Hosts or some secular godling. In order to attain and secure it, the modern hero will face three great tests—each involving an encounter with a transcendental aspect of ourselves which must be recognized and integrated: the robot, a mechanical replica of the primitive within us; the mutant, the threshold man of tomorrow, interlinking the animate and the inanimate and, at length, the *homo maximus*, the archetype of wholeness, the "universal soul which is also the soul of all men."[4]

Science fiction, which poses these and similar problems, represents a revival by other means of the alchemists' search for meaning in a world of explosive change. It is a crude attempt, resorting to the complete inventory of modern (and, in some instances, as yet non-existent) science and technology, to come to grips with the present state of terrestrial unrest and disorientation by relocating our inner conflicts in outer space and in times to come; to probe the whole universe, if need be, in pursuit of the elusive gods who once populated the heavens.

The viewpoint and mood are quite properly apocalyptic in response to the widespread, fervent desire for the genesis of a new world and the dawning of a new age—but the new mythology is not yet. Fighting the political battles and religious wars of our time in deep space and the far future cannot by itself put an end to anomie and alienation among individuals, restore ecological balance or devise foolproof formulas for dealing with global want and global fear.

We can no more pin our hopes on escapist fictions than on shopworn ideologies: on straight and narrow capitalism that strains and groans under the weight of its consumerist traditions and contradictions; on old-fashioned liberalism that pursues happiness by forever pouring out taxpayer's money; on communism and fascism that say that they can grow a human face despite the overwhelming evidence to the contrary.

For years, for decades—these various agendas have remained in effect in many places throughout the world; not because they are especially wise or of profound benefit to humankind but because those who challenged them failed to overcome the root problem of individual resistance to inner change.

In another day, more than forty years ago, President Roosevelt laid down an agenda which is as valid now as it was then. The Four Freedoms, he said, are the stuff of which democracy is made.[5] They are intertwined and interdependent. Men and women cannot live a full and undiminshed life without them. In the intervening years, freedom of speech and religion have, for the most part, been safeguarded and sustained and want has to some extent been mitigated; but fear thus far has defied every attempt to conquer it.

Now if fear were merely a by-product or function of want, those who do not suffer want would never be afraid. But they are, since fear draws no distinction between rich and poor. In fact, it is the authentic 20th Century specter which haunts all five continents. Fear feeds on itself; it paralyzes, deranges and immobilizes. It has changed man into a servant, a prisoner of the vast, demonic weapons arsenals and the cold and undependable bureaucracies created to administer them. For fear of his neighbor, man is prepared to destroy and for fear of himself, to self-destruct—placing his own survival, that of his children, of the generations to come, of this very planet in jeopardy.

"Is there not, whatever the nature of one's particular God, an element of a sacrilege involved in the placing of all this at stake just for the sake of the comforts, the fears and the national rivalries of a single generation?" asks George Kennan. "Is there not a moral obligation to recognize in this very uniqueness of the habitat and nature of man the greatest of our moral responsibilities, and to make of ourselves, in our national personification, its guardians and protectors rather than its destroyers?"[6]

There are some who simply brush the survival issue aside, saying that anyone who admits to fear is a coward, a well-intentioned fool or useful idiot. Others proclaim, on supposedly good authority, that the human race is doomed; that the end is near, apocalypse and tribulation are just around the corner and that all of us had better prepare for the eventuality. Whatever motivates either of them—be it defiance, resignation or some subtle combination of the two—they are asking humankind to join them in a desperate gamble, or worse still, a suicide pact.

The Four Freedoms, on the other hand, symbolize a covenant or compact between the citizen and his government; a kind of master plan to achieve emancipation. If this compact ever matured; if the convenant were honored, the New Man might at last emerge: he would no longer tremble and would no longer be torn this way and that as the theology student was in his dream of the two magicians. He would not be perfect; but he would be a whole man, a "finished soul,"[7] as Ralph Waldo Emerson has said.

Seen in this light, it is safe to say that the Four Freedoms are not only intertwined and interdependent but consecutive, like the rungs of a ladder; cumulative stages in a process of awareness. Each builds on the other and the wisdom of the entire structure lies in the perception that the soundness, sanity and, indeed, survival of society depend on the degree to which it manages to contend with its fears.

This is no deep dark secret. Those outside the mainstream whom society ostracizes, excludes or simply ignores can feel it: the expendable young and the disposable old; all the men and women who are not treated as equals; the working people for whom there are no jobs and those whose jobs deprive them of their spirit and soul—without regard to race, color, creed or political persuasion. Even the elect of society—the technicians, professionals and bureaucrats whose lives are less than full—can feel that there is too little soul and too much fear and that the common middle ground is largely missing.

Freedom from fear does not come cheaply; it is not won by a ruse or all at once. Prevailing over fear is like recovering from an illness; like regaining self-control and self-reliance; like being born again. It permits a man, a woman, a people, an entire nation to see things in a new light and provides the powers and skills to institute the changes that are long overdue.

There is a need for emancipation—as there was more than 100 years ago. No one can say just how many slaves the original Proclamation did set free; but it plainly signaled a fundamental shift in direction, if not an entirely new era in American history. Its psychological impact throughout the world and through the years attests to that.

The promise of the Proclamation itself, of the Constitutional Amendments and legislative acts passed since that time has not been fulfilled. Both blacks and whites are still half-slave and half-free in many respects—captives of a tenacious and enduring system which has never yet taught them that emancipation is a two-way street.

There has been movement, it is true; the ice has broken in places; but thus far there is no real cause for rejoicing. Blacks will only be free when whites attain to their full humanity and thereby become free themselves at last. But this act of joint and mutual liberation can only come about through an act of love, says the American theologian Robert MacAfee Brown; a "love that takes sides, love that seeks to pull down evil structures so that it can build up people no longer dominated and dehumanized by those structures, no matter on which side of the oppressor-oppressed dialectic they began."[8]

This is still another way of saying that America must put its divided house in order before it can begin to set examples for others to follow: that it must first know its own mind and heart and soul before it can develop a new vision which not merely "transcends the old political framework of left versus right" and "establishes a sound, sustainable economic system," as Fritjof Capra and Charlene Spretnak propose,[9] but one which truly transcends its self-imposed limits to spiritual growth.

Americans, no less than other peoples, have had their opportunities for such growth. One which was particularly auspicious emerged during the first half of the 19th century under the very name of Transcendentalism, an "intuitional religious, aesthetic, philosophical and ethical movement...a new humanism based upon ancient classical or Neo-Platonic supernaturalism and colored by Oriental mysticism."[10]

The mission of the Transcendentalists, as stated by Orestes Brownson, was one of peace, love and mediation. "In philosophy, theology, government, art, industry," he wrote in 1836, "we are to conciliate hostile feelings, and harmonize conflicting principles and interests. We must bind together the past and the future, reconcile progress and immobility; enable philosophy and theology to walk together in peace and love."[11]

To their own movement the Transcendentalists did not assign the color green, nor did they call it holistic as is the fashion today. But judging by what they said, wrote and felt and the causes they fought for (emancipation, among others), their primary goal was to preserve the physical and spiritual heritage of the ages, to build bridges between the past and the future and between the inner realm and the outer.

REFERENCES

1. Margaret Mead, *Continuities in Cultural Evolution*. (New Haven and London: Yale University Press, 1964), pp. 323-324.

2. C. G. Jung, *Flying Saucers: A Modern Myth* in Collected Works, vol. x. (Princeton, NJ: Princeton University Press, 1970), p. 343.

3. Ibid., p. 325f.

4. C. G. Jung, *Adam and Eve* in Collected Works, vol. xiv. (Princeton, NJ: Princeton University Press, 1970), p. 409.

5. Franklin D. Roosevelt's *Four Freedoms Speech* in Henry Steele Commager, *Documents of American History*. (New York: Appleton-Century-Crofts, 1958), pp. 626-629.

6. George F. Kennan, *Morality and Foreign Policy*. (Foreign Affairs, vol. 64, No. 2, Winter 1985/86).

7. William H. Gilman, J. E. Parsons, eds. *The Journals and Miscellaneous Notebooks of Ralph Waldo Emerson*. (Cambridge, MA: Harvard University Press, 1970), vol. 8, p. 380.

8. Robert MacAfee Brown, *Theology in a New Key*. (Philadelphia: Westminister Press, 1978), p. 149.

9. Fritjof Capra and Charlene Spretnak, *Green Politics*. (New York: E. P. Dutton, 1985), pp. xix-xx.

10. Kenneth Cameron, *Young Emerson's Transcendental Vision*. (Hartford, CN: Transcendental Books, 1971), p. 7.

11. Orestes A. Brownson, *Victor Cousin* in Perry Miller, *The Transcendentalists*. (Cambridge, MA: Harvard University Press, 1950), p. 114.

11
Emancipation and Convergence

> *There is no such thing as American science or Soviet science . . . Despite all the differences and controversies, all the scientists share common ideas: a respect for truth, a sense of moral responsibility, and a belief that the study of science and humanities can lead us to becoming truly multidimensional men and women of the future.*[1]

As the world continues to shrink and natural friends and natural enemies draw closer together, "the ideological spheres begin to touch, to interpenetrate, and the time may not be far off when the question of mutual understanding will become acute," Jung wrote in the late 1950s. "To make oneself understood is certainly impossible without comprehension of the other's standpoint. The insight needed for this will have repercussions on both sides. History will undoubtedly pass over those who feel it is their vocation to resist this inevitable development, however desireable and psychologically necessary it may be to cling to what is essential and good in our own tradition. Despite all the differences, the unity of mankind will assert itself irresistibly."[2]

For a time, this transformation may be thwarted by the holdfast powers of stasis and self-interest inherent in all societies. These days, their ideological bias is not so easy to identify or define as it once was. Left and right, reformers and conservatives, communists and capitalists seem to have formed shadow partnerships (beyond ideology) as they cling to the notion that man's control over the physical environment gives him control over his fate; that material progress and continued exploitation of natural resources will lead to better and better times; that armaments and high technology; advanced management techniques and social engineering can somehow be counted on to achieve global balance.

For all their convergent views regarding the physical world and how to deal with it, in matters of faith and political dogma the two camps still persist in resorting to invective to help perpetuate their differences. The vocabulary which keeps their tiresome war or words alive translates quite easily even while glossing over the conspicuous lack of insight and discrimination of both sides.

The appetite for projection and counter-projection will no doubt persist for some time to come. The relationship between the two superpowers may even degenerate periodically from cold war to permafrost. But we should not forget that there is a positive side to projection as well.

Psychologically speaking, projecting the image of a perceived adversary and providing him with a kind of hook on which to hang his own projections, indicates an unconscious desire to know more about him and, as it turns out, about oneself. In that sense, projection can be viewed as a first attempt at building a better, less encumbered relationship; the initial stage of a new common era.

Now, the projection phenomenon was not invented or discovered by 20th century psychology but has been common knowledge at least since Biblical times.[3] People were probably aware of it even before then and of the fact that withdrawal of projections stands to benefit the two parties involved by providing them with a middle ground; a meeting place where they might compose their differences.

The possibility does exist. In fact, the stirrings can be felt throughout the world—even in the very nations which are as unfree, regimented and totalitarian as any the 20th century has known. The shift in emphasis and mood is gradual and cautious; progress in the face of stubborn ideological bias is slow and uneven. But as Soviet dissident Zhores Medvedev predicted a number of years ago:

"In spite of the diversity of political regimes in society today and the differences in national traditions and customs, in spite of wide gaps between economic levels of countries, the inequality of distribution of poverty and riches over the globe, in the face of racial prejudices, the integration of mankind is undoubtedly taking place with ever-increasing speed and is the principal trend today—a social, political, economic and biological integration."[4]

The present, in other words, may still belong to the old guard; but the future will not, as the global village, wired for sight and sound, gradually becomes the locus of the conjunction of opposites; a free and open space—free of the gross anxieties, brutalities and famines of contemporary civilization.

As for today's superpowers, genuine convergence and fraternization will no doubt have to wait. The very governments which have been so slow and reluctant to reach sound and farsighted agreements over the years are unlikely to produce sudden miracles by the score; nor will they quickly overcome the need to project their deep-seated fears and most secret inadequacies (spiritual or otherwise) on each other. The Marxists, in other words, are not about to take Capitol Hill by storm and the capitalist lackeys will not be gaining ascendancy in the Kremlin any time soon. And yet, neither side may be able to resist or escape what may well turn out to be an inexorable convergence process predicated on the logic of history, on enlightened self-interest and the dawning recognition of joint responsibility for the future of the planet.

Moorhead Kennedy, one of the American diplomats held hostage in Tehran for more than a year, has put it as well as anyone. "Peace-making begins not with the Soviets or any other nation but among ourselves and within each of us," he writes. "It demands a willingness to respect the interests of others as well as our own, and to acknowledge a larger interest to which individual concerns are subordinate."[5]

It would surely be vain to search for, or claim to have discovered evidence of convergence where there is none or to base any hopes for such convergence on obvious similarities between the two superpowers such as land mass, revolutionary origin, comradeship-in-arms and the common experience of post-industrial trauma; to postulate harmony and equilibrium for its own sake—in short, to indulge in wishful thinking. But it is equally inappropriate to view mere willingness to contemplate the potential benefits to be gained from such developments as a betrayal of the perceived fundamental values of either side or to deny the inherent dynamics of such processes simply out of fear of confrontation and possible contamination.

"Our own cold warriors have always insisted that détente must await the reform of the Soviet system," writes Princeton political scientist Stephen Cohen. "But that ill-conceived policy serves only to undermine the reformist cause in the Soviet Union. It results in an inadvertent but perilous axis between their hard-liners and ours, an axis whose first victims are the advocates of Soviet reform. Thus, the struggle between the friends and foes of reform is also a struggle between the friends and foes of détente—in the Soviet Union and in the West. In the nuclear age, no more important lesson can be learned from the past or the present."[6]

As in the domestic sphere, this calls for the establishment and maintenance of viable coalitions of natural allies; groups which have outgrown the bifurcated world of yesterday and today and replaced it with a vision of the unified world of tomorrow. The cold warriors of both camps—the inheritors of Russian insularity and the heirs of American isolationism —are the natural enemies of tomorrow's world.

What the convergence phenomenon really seems to tell us is that we need each other, not as scapegoats or whipping boys, but in order to make the world safe—beyond sentimentalism, sensationalism, blind faith or blind ideology—not for democracy or communism but simply free, free from fear in Roosevelt's sense.

Given favorable conditions, therefore, and wiser leadership, less committed to brute strength and false pride, the priorities not only of individual men and women but even of entire nations might in time be restructured in conformance with ancient truths and the advanced insights into the sympathy of all things gathered by modern depth psychology and the new physics.

As documented in recent popular works by a number of authors,[7] the parallel explorations of "transcendental territory"[8] undertaken by these two disciplines—proceeding from different assumptions and employing differenct analytical methods—have resulted in the rediscovery of the image of a unitary world and man's role in it; validating and reinterpreting panoptic, ecumenical views held throughout the ages.

The world as the natural philosophers of the Renaissance and the alchemists saw it; the world which is even now reemerging from the haze of divided reality is/was one world, governed by a principle of universal vitalism which suggests, according to Cassirer, "that nature is not composed of parts, and does not fall into different classes of entities that are distinct in substance from each other...The universe is like a string under tension, which, touched at any point, propagates the disturbance in every direction so that it can be traced in every one of its parts."[9]

In Pico's universe, man acts as the connecting link between above and below, whose goal and purpose it is to restore the harmony of nature and, in the process, to transform himself. Man, Pico says, "is the bond and node of celestial and terrestrial. Neither of these can have peace with the other unless man is at peace with himself, for he ratifies their peace and treaty in himself."[10]

Modern physics seems perfectly at ease with this type of imagery. Using contemporary terminology in place of the more ornate language of the past, American nuclear physicist John Wheeler authenticates the linkage between man and the universe, individual and cosmos, observer and observed while leaving the underlying symbolism of their mutual involvement virtually intact:

"The quantum principle has demolished the once-held view that the universe sits safely 'out there,' that we can observe what goes on in it from behind a foot-thick slab of plate glass without ourselves being involved in what goes on. We have learned that to observe even so miniscule an object as an electron we have to shatter that glass. We have to reach out and insert a measuring device. We can install a device to measure position or insert a device to measure momentum; but the installation of the one prevents the insertion of the other. We ourselves have to decide which it is that we will do. Whichever it is, it has an unpredictable effect on the future of that electron, and to that degree the future of the universe is changed. We changed it. We have to cross out that old word 'observer' and replace it by the new word 'participator.' In some strange sense the quantum principle tells us that we are dealing with a participatory universe."[11]

The psychophysical world of mutual involvement as we know it today, liberated from its denatured state, awakened from its centuries-long slumber, represents the high ground where the opposites are reconciled; the interface of the "continuous 'spiritual circuit'…that leads from God to the world and from the world to God,"[12] as the art historian Erwin Panofsky has put it.

It is a kind of prefiguration of the *unus mundus*—or in Jung's words, the "potential world outside time, the eternal Ground of all empirical being…the relation or identity of the personal with the suprapersonal atman, and of the individual tao with the universal tao."[13]

REFERENCES

1. Wiktor Osiatynski, *Contrasts: Soviet and American Thinkers Discuss the Future*. (New York: MacMillan, 1985), pp. xvi, xvii.

2. C. G. Jung, *The Undiscovered Self* in Collected Works, vol. x. (Princeton, NJ: Princeton University Press, 1970), pp. 294-295.

3. Matthew 7:3.

4. Zhores Medvedev, *The Medvedev Papers*, trans. Vera Rich. (London: MacMillan, 1971), p. 255.

5. Moorhead Kennedy, *The Ayatollah in the Cathedral: Reflections of a Hostage*. (New York: Hill and Wang, 1986), p. 194.

6. Stephen F. Cohen, *Rethinking the Soviet Experience*. (New York and Oxford: Oxford University Press, 1985), p. 157.

7. Cf. Fritjof Capra, *The Turning Point*. (New York: Simon & Schuster, 1982); Amit Goswami, *The Cosmic Dancers*. (New York: Harper & Row, 1983); Ken Wilber, *Quantum Questions*. (Boulder and London: Shambhala, 1984).

8. C. G. Jung, *Aion*. (Princeton, NJ: Princeton University Press, 1979), p. 261.

9. Ernst Cassirer, *Giovanni Pico della Mirandola, A Study in the History of Reanissance Ideas*. (Journal of the History of Ideas, vol. 3, No. 3, June, 1942), p. 338.

10. Giovanni Pico della Mirandola, *Heptaplus*, v., 7 in Avery Dulles, *Princeps Concordiae*. (Cambridge, MA: Harvard University Press, 1941), p. 116.

11. John Wheeler, *The Universe as Home for Man*. (American Scientist, vol. 62, Nov/Dec 1974), p. 689.

12. Erwin Panofsky, *Renaissance and Renascences in Western Art*. (Copenhagen: Russak & Co., 1960), p. 183.

13. C. G. Jung, *The Conjunction* in Collected Works, vol. xiv. (Princeton, NJ: Princeton University Press, 1970), pp. 534, 535.

12

The Anatomy of Transformation

> *Psychology is just as little a substitute for religion as personal experience is a replacement for knowledge through faith. However, the great significance of psychology is to enable the individual to understand the opposites within himself and to help him bear his destined limitations.*[1]

The question, as always, is how to get there from here and, as always, there is no single easy answer. Throughout these pages, we have been hypothesizing that 20th century depth psychology might provide at least part of it; that C. G. Jung's encompassing view of modern humanity might serve as a benchmark or significant point of reference for the future.

Conventional psychology, by contrast, is more likely to concentrate on specifics, upholding its commitment to the mechanistic axioms in vogue at the turn of this century when pioneers such as Freud and Adler first postulated that sexuality and unbridled personal ambition are the drives which make the (Western) world go round.

In certain respects, progressive vulgarization of their original theories has reduced psychology and psycholanalysis to a kind of middle-class entertainment and the couch to a launching pad from which these and other drives may be propelled into orbit. Although their release is apt to make for a realignment of psychic energy, there is no assurance whatever that this will bring about genuine fulfillment and equilibrium. If it did, far fewer people today would be as troubled, lonely and suicidal as they are—turning to addictive substances, prepackaged spirituality and the relentless pursuit of material ends to allay their fears, fill out their empty lives and desensitize their souls.

In fact—now, at the end of the century, three generations of analysts and patients later, the primary focus still seems to be on sexuality and power and there still are many men and women who do their utmost to avoid the encounter with the wide-open spaces of the spirit and soul. And yet, the manifest destiny—not only of Americans—would seem to lie along that very road to the interior.

Although Jung saw no reason to dispute the importance attached to the two drives, he believed that the roots of the modern dilemma lay deeper—beyond the pleasure principle and even beyond discontent with civilization; that the needs of modern men and women were/are in the first instance spiritual.

"The crux of the spiritual problem today is to be found in the fascination which the psyche holds for modern man," Jung wrote. "If we are pessimistic, we shall call it a sign of decadence; if we are optimistically inclined, we shall see in it the promise of a far-reaching spiritual change in the Western world. At all events, it is a significant phenomenon. It is the more noteworthy because it is rooted in the deeper social strata, and the more important because it touches those irrational and—as history shows—incalculable psychic forces which transform the life of peoples and civilizations in ways that are unforeseen and unforeseeable."[2]

Jung's basic premise was that genuine change can only come from within. The central issue for our day and age, he stressed therefore, is to resolve inner conflict and create balance; to find meaning and increase awareness to the fullest extent possible; to recognize both one's uniqueness in all its aspects and one's indissoluble kinship with the whole of humankind. This dual experience certainly encompasses a great deal of Jung's concept of individuation.

Leonardo Boff, the Brazilian theologian, characterizes individuation as "the longest and most perilous journey made by human beings in search of the center that attracts, polarizes and harmonizes all."[3]

Jungian psychologist Esther Harding points out that individuation is "a modern term for that process by which the individual progresses toward completeness and becomes truly man."[4]

Jung himself conceived of individuation as a natural process which unfolds in keeping with ancient and immutable patterns. Each living thing, in order to fulfill its particular design and purpose, will eventually become what it inherently is and always was: "An acorn becomes an oak, the calf a cow, and the child an adult."[5]

Precisely because of this attribute of naturalness which allows the process to unfold, as it were, autonomously, the average person will ordinarily take little or no heed of it, becoming aware of it only when an impasse is reached; when the path to the future seems blocked. It is in this bleak and hopeless hour that the individual is likely to hear a higher summons to proceed into the inner darkness.

And it is then that a subtle shift of gravity is likely to occur: the ego's hold over the personality relaxes; the blinding light emitted by it grows fainter and in the distance we begin to make out the contours of the bigger man or woman who dwells within us. Jung has called this inner guiding factor, superordinate to the ego, the self—the new center which, like a magnet, "attracts to itself that which is proper to it...i.e., everything that pertains to the orginal and unalterable character of the individual ground plan."⁶

The prime element of that ground plan (and the individuation process as such) is the establishment and maintenance of a link between the ego, the locus of human consciousness, and the self, the expression of the total psyche (which includes both the conscious and the unconscious); the locus of the conjunction of opposites. Like God, the self can be experienced but is essentially unknowable and as the earth revolves around the sun, so the ego circumambulates the self.

"Often one has the impression that the personal psyche is running around this point central like a shy animal," Jung Jung says, "at once fascinated and frightened, always in flight and yet steadily drawing nearer."⁷

The secret (if indeed it is one) is not to inhibit or arrest the process but to merge with its rhythm and flow and recapture the long-forgotten language of myths, dreams and fairy tales; to let nature be nature. Man, the earth (and presumably the universe) are concentric biospheres kept in balance by archetypal forces which to beings with our particular lifespan cannot but appear eternal.

"The same physiological and psychological processes that have been man's for hundreds of thousands of years still endure, instilling in our inmost hearts this profound intuition of the 'eternal' continuity of the living. But the self, as an inclusive term that embraces our whole living organism, not only contains the deposit and totality of all past life, but is also a point of departure from which all future life will spring."⁸

To let nature be nature under such conditions is the better part of wisdom—both in the Eastern sense of letting things be and embracing unembraceable infinity and, in the Western sense of being aware of the polarities inherent in these connected systems and making the effort to endure the resultant pulls and strains.

Endurance, in fact, is probably the crux of the matter; a willingness to carry the sprouting seeds that have been planted to full term. But endurance does not merely suggest the ability to wait—for Godot; for a convincing reinterpretation of our existential situation—but also the courage to overcome the impasse Western civilization seems to have reached and to admit (to ourselves) that the need for religion in the dual sense of being grounded and being able to soar beyond workaday concerns and constrictions is compelling, global and virtually irresistible. This need may be met in a variety of ways, but in all instances we humans—until further notice—will be the ones who are contained, like our home planet earth, in a larger system; a system whose nebulous expansiveness and whose protective umbrella we can feel but at whose inner and outer limits we can merely guess.

"The symbols of divinity coincide with those of the self," Jung writes. "What on the one side, appears as a psychological experience signifying psychic wholeness, expresses on the other side the idea of God. This is not to assert a metaphysical identity of the two, but merely the empirical identity of the images representing them, which all originate in the human psyche."[9]

Whenever human beings are fortunate enough to attain that state of dynamic equilibrium—the Church calls it grace—when they and the image after which they were made momentarily overlap, they gain something of an insight into their own full potential and the essential nature of their creator: as a child may fleetingly intuit what its parent's imprint on it has been and, based on that perception, infer what that parent is truly like.

By transcending the traditional theological and psychological definitions of the primordial, compensatory relationship between God and humankind; by stating, as he does elsewhere, that "anyone who wants to can at least draw near to the source of such experiences, no matter whether he believes in God or not,"[10] Jung reveals himself as an authentic guide and mentor, showing the humanists among us how to bridge the gap to religious experience and the religious among us how to reconcile their perceptions with the humanist view of the world.

Like any body of thought; like any psycho-philosophical or psycho-religious theory, that of Jung can be turned into a cult complete with a quasi-secret, quasi-occult language of its own and a single-minded, however small, army of devotees. The house that Jung built then runs the risk of being taken for a shrine, a monument to the oddities of the human spirit, and his writings for a treasure trove of inerrant profundities.

"Games" such as these, entered for personal gain, may provide solipsistic gratification; but as in the case of the self-seekers of another day who took the alchemists' writings literally the end product may well turn out to be nothing but fool's gold.

Individuation and individualism have little or nothing in common. In fact, the two are as far apart today as they were in Pico's time: they represent the high and low roads to personal fulfillment. Individualism is one of the major symbols of our time, appearing as greed, self-advancement and gluttony in a great many walks of life and a great many relationships, including those which are meant to be most intimate.

As the individual pursues his or her own ends at practically any cost, infatuated with material goals, satisfying biological wants, neglecting the needs of his less developed inner world, society as a whole loses, social responsibility breaks down, the sense of community disintegrates and the individual himself, obsessed with conquest and domination, comes away empty-handed and alone.

"It cannot possibly be the object of human education," says Jung, "to create an anarchic conglomeration of individual existences. That would be too much like the unavowed ideal of extreme individualism, which is essentially no more than a morbid reaction against an equally futile collectivism. In contrast to all this, the natural process of individuation brings to birth a consciousness of human community precisely because it makes us aware of the unconscious, which unites and is common to all mankind."[11]

For modern Western men and women, who all too often respond to the world and to life at a remove, on the outside looking in, or as aliens in a cage, that grand connection is tenuous, provided it still exists at all. The systematic slaughter of millions here, there and everywhere on orders of cruel dictators and callous generals; the random decimation of communities, tribes and entire nations as a result of drought, famine, ruthless exploitation or mere benign neglect has given birth to generation after generation of nonbelievers in the philanthropy of God and the immortality of the human soul. The transitory, repetitive character of life on earth under virtually all political, social and economic systems has been the cause of fashionable or genuine boredom, insensitivity and despair.

And whereas our Western doubts about the existence of a higher being and about life without him (or her) impinge on our peace of mind, the global underclass which encircles and far outnumbers us is plagued not only by spiritual hunger and homelessness but by the excruciating harshness of daily life and daily death in a political and economic underworld from which, for the millions, there appears to be no escape.

Neither for them, nor for us will the spiritual uplift and nourishment we all need come from the dogmatic and traditional formulas of the past. In our part of the world, a life spent in some orthodox pursuit, giving serious offense to no one, acquiring the requisite amount of treasure and dispensing the requisite amount of affection and support will not, because it cannot, suffice to turn seekers and spiritual indigents into rounded and grounded men and women, properly equipped to deal with the personal and collective complexities of modern life. And in that other part of the world, the lackluster teachings and preachings of the conventional churches will not free the landless, jobless, penniless masses from age-old bondage and dependency or provide the true impetus for a great leap forward. For them, as for us, the time is ripe, overripe for *aggiornamento*, the application of present-day methods to present-day problems.

Boff believes that "we are living in privileged times."[12] His reason for feeling as he does is that "there is an upsurge of life in the [Catholic] Church that is revitalizing the entire body from head to toe."[13] Boff, of course, is referring to the strength and momentum of Third World liberation theology which seeks to minister to the spiritual needs of the pauperized masses even as it supports their efforts to overcome the harsh political, social and economic systems under which they must live.

Interestingly enough, the tenor of Boff's recent statement very nearly matches that of an observation made by Jung some thirty years ago.

"We are living in what the Greeks called the *kairos*," he wrote, "the right moment for a 'metamorphosis of the gods,' of fundamental principles and symbols. This peculiarity of our time, which is certainly not of our conscious choosing, is the expression of the unconscious man within us who is changing."[14]

Liberation theology may well provide one set of answers, for those of us who are trapped in the ranks of the world underclass. Jungian psychology may provide another, for those of us who have virtually everything they need except genuine faith.

The two responses cannot and must not be equated, nor should liberation theology be used (or misused) as an easy vehicle to convey Western nonbelievers to the next higher spiritual plateau. In order to reach our own future, we will have to rely on our own spiritual resources and our own means of transport.

Still, there is an underlying theme common to both which ought not to be overlooked: the awareness—so as not to say conviction—that humankind is at a turning point, poised at the threshold of a new age, and that the liberation of the individual is the first, indispensable step on the way to a freer world.

The two contexts out of which this perception of fundamental change has grown are markedly different; the response to human anguish is unquestionably based on different experiences and levels of deprivation; the premises and priorities are as divergent as they are bound to be when the world is viewed from the far side of the great North-South divide in one case and from the safe haven of well-to-do Switzerland on the other.

But when all is said and done, there is no escaping the fact that we are really all in it together—nonbelievers and nonpersons, whatever our spiritual antecedents; rich and poor, whatever the color of our skin; that we are all entitled to the same rights and privileges, subject to the same laws and commandments; aspiring to the same goals; confronted with the same existential tasks and prospects; endowed with the same human dignity.

"Today, we live in a unitary world," Jung wrote, "where distances are reckoned by hours and no longer by weeks and months. Exotic races . . . have become our neighbors, and what was yesterday the private concern of the ethnologist is today a political, social and psychological problem."[15]

REFERENCES

1. Liliane Frey-Rohn, *From Freud to Jung*. (New York: Putnam, 1974), p. 305.

2. C. G. Jung, *The Spiritual Problem of Modern Man* in Collected Works, vol. x. (Princeton, NJ: Princeton University Press, 1970), p. 92.

3. Leonardo Boff, *Jesus Christ Liberator*, trans. Patrick Hughes. (Maryknoll, NY: Orbis Books, 1978), pp. 240-241.

4. M. Esther Harding, *Psychic Energy: Its Source and Its Transformation*. (Princeton, NJ: Princeton University Press, 1963), p. 308.

5. C. G. Jung, *Answer to Job* in Collected Works, vol. xi. (Princeton, NJ: Princeton UniversityPress, 1969), p. 468.

6. C. G. Jung, *Aion*. (Princeton, NJ: Princeton University Press, 1979), p. 190.

7. C. G. Jung, *Individual Dream Symbolism in Relation to Alchemy* in Collected Works, vol, xii. (Princeton, NJ: Princeton University Press, 1968), p. 218.

8. C. G. Jung, *The Relations Between the Ego and the Unconscious: Anima and Animus* in Collected Works, vol. vii. (New York: Pantheon, 1953), p. 190.

9. C. G. Jung, *Flying Saucers: A Modern Myth* in Collected Works, vol. x. (Princeton, NJ: Princeton University Press, 1970), p. 339.

10. C. G. Jung, *The Undiscovered Self* in Collected Works, vol. x. (Princeton, NJ: Princeton University Press, 1970), p. 293.

11. C. G. Jung, *Psychotherapy Today* in Collected Works, vol. xvi. (New York: Pantheon, 1954), p. 108.

12. Leonardo Boff, *Church: Charism and Power* [tr. John W. Diercksmeyer]. (New York: Crossroad, 1985), p. ix.

13. Ibid.

14. C. G. Jung, *The Undiscovered Self* in Collected Works, vol. x. (Princeton, NJ: Princeton University Press, 1970), p. 304.

15. Ibid., p. 294

13
Thresholds and Crossings

> *The memories of well over a hundred thousand years of speech have been coded into the molecules which are inherent in all the cells of the body. This is the resurrection: the fact that the dead move among us the living; with their accomplishments alive in our flesh.*[1]

In the fall of 1909, Jung traveled to the United States in the company of Sigmund Freud and some of his disciples to deliver several lectures at Clark University in Worcester, Massachusetts. On that trip, Jung had a powerful and significant dream he would remember for the rest of his life.[2]

It took place in a two-story house. Though Jung had no recollection of ever having set foot in it before, he somehow knew that the house was his. The upstairs was elegantly furnished in rococo style; but on the ground level the furniture was medieval and the floor was of red brick. Exploring the house further, Jung came upon a vaulted room in the cellar which evidently dated from Roman times, and when he lifted up a stone slab in the cellar floor, he discovered still another set of stairs leading down.

"I descended, and entered a low cave cut into the rock. Thick dust lay on the floor, and in the dust were scattered bones and broken pottery, like remains of a primitive culture."[3]

At that point, Jung woke up; the "big dream" was finished. It had presented him with a faithful, albeit symbolic portrait of himself; the healer of souls as archeologist: going backward in time, digging for roots and relics; making explicit what is implicit in the origins and memories of man. The dream, he said later, was "a kind of structural diagram of the human psyche . . . a history of successive layers of consciousness."[4]

The house, in other words, was the dwelling place of what he came to call the archetypes—the images, agents and forces which, as part of the universal experience of living, have left their cumulative and indelible imprint on our psyche.

The uppermost floor manifestly stood for consciousness; the succeeding levels of the house took Jung further and further down into the unconscious; into the cave "world of the primitive man within myself,"[5] the common (burial) ground of all our human and animal ancestors. Jung's psyche had chosen well: the house image was indeed felicitous and to the point. What the dream told him was that this house of many rooms and many levels would remain a house divided unless the upper and lower halves were accorded equal attention and treated with equal care.

"Conscious and unconscious do not make a whole when one of them is suppressed and injured by the other. If they must contend, let it at least be a fair fight with equal rights on both sides. Both are aspects of life. Consciousness should defend its reason and protect itself, and the chaotic life of the unconscious should be given the chance of having its way too—as much of it as we can stand. This means open conflict and open collaboration at once. That, evidently, is the way human life should be. It is the old game of hammer and anvil: between them the patient iron is forged into an indestructible whole, an 'individual.' This, roughly, is what I mean by the individuation process."[6]

Professional and popular literature abound with accounts of successful and not-so-successful individuation experiences. The separate life stories may be convoluted or straightforward and the tellers of these stories may or may not succeed in stirring the reader by providing him with insights into his or her own psyche. But however unique the individual story may be, the underlying patterns never change. The reason, as Jungian analyst June Singer points out, is not hard to find:

"We carry with us not only the drives and repressions of our personal histories, but also the weight of centuries of tradition, of belief, of fears and of expectations...conditioned not only by our parents and the members of our generation but by the archetypal parents who make themselves known in myths as kings and queens, gods and goddesses, the sun and the moon, the demons and the muses."[7]

In a typical individuation process, one of the first archetypes encountered is the one which in myth and fiction often appears as a companion, confederate or *Doppelgaenger*. In Jungian parlance, this dim, veiled brother or sister of the conscious mind is known as the "shadow," representing the dark or far side one cannot or will not see: all the repressed traits and rejected options; all the unfulfilled promises.

From a rational, intellectual point of view, the idea of the shadow is not very hard to grasp. Parents, pastors and educators tell us in so many words what he is like from the time they think we are old enough to take it to heart. And whenever we break the rules in later life or overstep our limits, someone is always there to remind us of that imperfect, untamed lesser man or woman we take such pains to conceal. It gives us no joy to hear it; but in our soul we do know what they mean. In fact, we are quite aware—sporadically, though by no means always—of the contradictory and incompatible elements within us.

The instinctive reaction and response to this dilemma is to find still more effective ways of camouflaging that shadowy, shady half of ours, hiding it from ourselves, if not from others; holding it on a leash, censoring it in order to create the illusion—at least in our own mind—that we are always right and others are always wrong. This, in turn, permits the shadow to grow at the expense of our consciousness of him—a familiar experience on the personal and collective level.

"The historic events of our time have painted a picture of man's psychic reality in indelible colors of blood and fire," Jung wrote in one of his darker moods, "and given him an object lesson which he will never be able to forget if—and that is the great question—he has today acquired enough consciousness to keep up with the furious pace of the devil within him."[8]

The shadow problem offers a moral choice and the most promising chance for moral survival to the individual (and to society as a whole). The need, therefore, to come to grips (and to terms) with it may and often does become imperative, as personal experience and world history amply demonstrate.

The Germans must wrestle with the demons of their Nazi past just as Americans must confront the many-headed monster that is or was Vietnam, Antietam, or, indeed, Wounded Knee. The realization that wrestler and demon, wrestler and monster are a secret and congenital twosome is like a door opening to a distinctly new prospect. Still, the shadow can no more be domesticated than was Caliban by Prospero. But, like all the archetypes, he can guide us deeper into the interior, if we let him.

"This confrontation," says Jung, "is the first test of courage on the inner way, a test sufficient to frighten off most people, for the meeting with ourselves belongs to the more unpleasant things that can be avoided so long as we can project everything negative into the environment. But if we are able to see our own shadow and can bear knowing about it, then a small part of the problem has already been solved."[9]

This giant step (for humankind) which solves a small part of the problem always requires a hero, whose task, in mythology, is to redeem the timeless covenant and put a whole universe back in order. In a more mundane setting, contemporary men and women, embarked on the search for the key which fits their own particular door, are confronted with the no less daunting task of restoring the archetypal connection between their ego and the self.

Like the heroes of old, they must be willing and indeed fearless enough to take upon themselves the burdens and hardships and the loneliness of their individual way. Like the heroes, they must go out to fight dragons and sea monsters, bring life back to the wasteland; unhorse the black knight and free the captive princess. And like them, they will revolutionize even as they restore, raising themselves and their orbit to a higher state of awareness—bringing down the old and bringing on the new, where the new invariably turns out to be an enriched and transcending version of the old.

It stands to reason that these tests, trials and triumphs must not be viewed intellectually or taken literally: the storybook hero wielding his magic sword or using his bare hands to do what has to be done is none other, of course, than our better self, joining battle with the forces that would keep us from attaining wholeness.

The myths and archetypes, in other words, speak to us in a symbolic language of their own which has a direct bearing not only on our individual reality but on the collective concerns of mankind: on human rights and the equitable distribution of wealth and resources; on global rivalries, on the nuclear age and nuclear holocaust.

They call on us to act; to rebuild the world of symbols—because sloth and unknowing will simply leave the world as it is and theatrics will merely transform it into a fool's paradise. Good advice, subtle pressure, even brute force will not make adversaries or enemies—real or imaginary—change their minds and their evil ways. The fact is that nothing will really change unless individuals change; only then will a ripple effect occur—or as Heinrich Zimmer, the Indologist, has put it: "Change yourself (that is the lesson), and you inhabit a renovated world."[10] This above all is the meaning of the politics of individuation.

Certainly, one way of looking at individuation would be to say that, under the best of circumstances, it overcomes the various states of incompleteness which characterize the human situation: the state of dissociation from one's shadow side, from one's contrasexual component and from the God-image or self. It is the inner urge toward completeness, toward uniting the multiplicity of opposites which starts the process on its way and keeps it going.

The androgyny phenomenon, the subject of so much current interest and concern, has increased awareness of the fact that the character of men is not entirely masculine and that of women is not entirely feminine. Modern biology has found that it is the greater presence of male or female genes, as the case may be, which determines the sex of a child. And modern psychology, following in the footsteps of ancient wisdom and the Renaissance concept of balance and complementarity, has shown that what is apparent on the surface is matched—as it must be—by something else which is hidden within.

In Jungian psychology, the woman hidden within, in a man's unconscious, is referred to as the *anima* and the hidden man in woman is called *animus*. In the everyday world of human relations, the two are generally experienced as projected images—visible but not assimilable; manifesting themselves "out there" but not as yet "in here."

Their potential role, however, is that of mediator or mediatrix between the two psychic realities; helping to bridge the gap between the individual ego and the archetypal world of the unconscious and to pave the way to what Jung has called "the ultimate phase of the work . . . the union of opposites in the archetypal form of the *hierosgamos* or 'chymical wedding.' Here, the supreme opposites, male and female (as in the Chinese *yang* and *yin*), are melted into a unity purified of all opposition and therefore incorruptible."[11]

The common element of this sacred conjunction in alchemy and mythology, in fairy tales and dreams is that a symbolic balance has been struck by linking up with the essential content—feminine or masculine—which until then had been conspicuous by its absence and elusiveness.

The centuries of male domination and the understandable excitement and elation over the gradual and progressive liberation of women have tended to obscure the fact that emancipation really belongs to and is required by all—men and women alike. But in order to reach that state of equality and independence in social, economic and political life, we must first resolve the incongruities in our own inner realm. Once that has been achieved, society as a whole may benefit—for as the individual goes, so goes the nation and, for that matter, the world.

To be sure, there are no quick and easy solutions or home remedies for our many psychic defects and moral disorders. The road to individuation is narrow, arduous and long. It moves through successive stages of discrimination and refinement and is contingent both on the amount of psychological energy available at each juncture and the capacity of the conscious mind to retain possession of the new insights it continually acquires. Throughout, the ego circles around the midpoint, drawn by the magnetic field of the self; motivated by the urge to fulfill its individual ground plan.

"The beginnings of our whole psychic life seem to be inextricably rooted in this point," says Jung, "and all our highest and ultimate purposes seem to be striving towards it."[12]

Why this is so, we do not know. All we can say is that we feel the pull and seem to hear the call. It may well be that certain animals are not alone in having a homing instinct; that we human beings are similarly endowed, with a sixth sense that directs us toward the center and origin of things again and again, to roost, to brood, to seek ultimate meaning.

"The announcements of the soul," Emerson wrote in one of his essays, "are always attended by the emotion of the sublime. For this communication is an influx of the Divine into our mind. It is an ebb of the individual rivulet before the flowing surges of the sea of life. Every distinct apprehension of this central commandment agitates men with awe and delight."[13]

Since all cultures, civilizations and creeds have been touched by the self in their own particular way, the names given to this higher dimension of the spirit are many. But wherever we may live—in the city, in the desert, in the jungle or the rain forest—we know the feeling of being at one with oneself, one's fellow human beings and the natural world within and without us. It is a catholic experience in the sense of being all-pervasive and universal; it is democratic because it is freely available to all and it is emancipatory in the sense of making free men and women of every one of us.

REFERENCES

1. John Bleibtreu, *The Parable of the Beast*, (New York: MacMillan, 1968), p. 89.

2. C. G. Jung, *Memories, Dreams, Reflections* recorded and edited by Aniela Jaffé. (New York: Random House, 1965), pp. 158-159.

3. Ibid.

4. Ibid., p. 161.

5. Ibid., p. 160.

6. C. G. Jung, *Conscious, Unconscious and Individuation* in Collected Works, vol. ix, part 1. (Princeton, NJ: Princeton University Press, 1971), p. 288.

7. June Singer, *Androgyny*. (Garden City, NJ: Doubleday, 1976), pp. 264-265.

8. C. G. Jung, *The Spirit Mercurius* in Collected Works, vol. xiii, (Princeton, NJ: Princeton University Press, 1967), p. 244.

9. C. G. Jung, *Archetypes of the Collective Unconscious* in Collected Works, vol. ix., part 1. (Princeton, NJ: Princeton University Press, 1968), p. 20.

10. Heinrich Zimmer, *The King and the Corpse*. (Princeton, NJ: Princeton University Press, 1971), p. 231.

11. C. G. Jung, *Introduction to the Religious and Psychological Problems of Alchemy* in Collected Works, vol. xii. (Princeton, NJ: Princeton University Press, 1968), p. 43.

12. C. G. Jung, *The Mana Personality* in Collected Works, vol. vii. (New York: Pantheon, 1953), p. 236.

13. Ralph Waldo Emerson, "The Over-Soul" in *Selected Writings*. (New York: Random House, 1950), p. 269.

14
The Archetype of Futurity

> *The community today is the planet, not the bounded nation; hence the patterns of projected aggression which formerly served to coordinate the ingroup now can only break it into factions. The national idea, with the flag as totem . . . and the numerous saints of this anticult—namely the patriots whose ubiquitous photographs, draped with flags, serve as official icons—are precisely the local threshold guardians whom it is the first problem of the hero to surpass.*[1]

In the Jungian scheme of things, individuation is a lifelong growth process; a sequence of initiation rites which guide and accompany men and women through the successive stages of life. During the first half of life, which ordinarily is devoted to assuming one's role in society, the doors open to the world outside. During the second half of life, the doors tend to lead to the interior.

It is with this latter process of consolidation and adjustment to inner realities and inner needs that Jung was primarily concerned. But today the boundary lines between the generations and the first and second half of life are far more fluid than they used to be and, as a consequence, the multiple existential problems of our time confront both young and old with equal severity, granting immunity to no one.

In more traditional societies, the divisions of human life still are quite faithfully observed. The young are cherished as bearers of a bright future; the old are venerated as custodians of a bountiful past. Each age group: the young seeker, the householder, the contemplative and the aged wise man, as in the ideal Indian formula, has its foreordained and indispensable role to play. The very existence of society depends on it.

But in the modern (Western) world, that social contract has all but expired. The generations are out of touch with each other and, for the most part, with their natural roles as well. The young no longer glow with the freshness of great expectations; the old no longer shine with the ripeness of fulfillment. And the age groups in between are trapped in a grey area—afraid of dying and afraid, too, of living life to the full.

Questions about life already lived, life yet to be lived and unlived life never to be recaptured are apt to arise at some significant turning point, such as in midlife. But today, the furious tempo of life, which compresses vicarious and actual experiences of a lifetime into mere decades and the psychic shocks of decades into a few short years, forces the young—psychologically prepared or not—to deal with these same questions at a much earlier stage of development.

One particular phenomenon of which the members of the present generation are supremely aware is that the world is shrinking even as they add to their years. They are growing up, learning, studying, working, living in Marshall McLuhan's "electrically configured world...a world not of wheels but of circuits, not of fragments but of integral patterns."[2]

They may never have heard of Jung, of depth psychology, the archetypes and all the rest, but they can surely feel that the process in which they are caught up extends far beyond the mere dynamics of political and economic change; that they are, for better or worse, the beneficiaries of a world revolution which is based on no specific ideology but fundamentally affects their perception of themselves, their neighbors and the world around them.

It may be useful to recall in this context that these are the very same young people who have had full exposure to the sweep and thrust of the catastrophic events of our age; to matters of life and death on a global scale from the time they were first able to read, write and watch television.

These experiences, however vicarious and fragmented they may be, have taught them not only to fear for their own personal safety and the survival of the species but have also alerted them to the diminished relevance and efficacy of yesterday's political doctrines, religious practices and social attitudes that are still being passed on to them in the guise of a precious and immutable inheritance. But for all their heightened awareness and deep skepticism, it seems they have yet to decide where to turn in their search for an effective and meaningful formula to fill the political and spiritual vacuum.

At this critical juncture, Jung can help make their choice easier by providing a realistic alternative—not a new cult or religion; not a political platform or economic and social agenda, but a design for the future which liberates the inner and the outer man (or woman), the society as a whole and, by extension, the world-at-large.

In the first instance, Jung was a doctor and healer; an empiricist in the humanist mold and tradition, an experimenter drawn onward by profound curiosity and kept within bounds by scientific discipline; a discoverer and explorer who sought answers for this age which might retain their validity in the next and serve as a seedbed for continued growth.

It is this forward-looking and at the same time conservative aspect of Jung's work and world view which might well speak to the members of today's generation, whose need for an anchor is as evident as their restless urge to move ahead.

The dawning Age of Aquarius, Jung believed, "will constellate the problem of the union of opposites."[3] To anyone living today, this may well sound both like a fond hope and a foregone conclusion. The split within and without which is causing such harm and anguish throughout the world is plain to see. It cannot widen indefinitely without tearing us all apart. And yet, concurrently, there is a unitary world growing up all around us which tells us that there are various forces at work—in science, in technology, in communications, even in political life—apparently intent on healing that very split.

This is not to say that the scientists and politicians have a specific remedy for our woes and aches ready and waiting for us; that they merely need to be nudged and cajoled into revealing the secret prescription they have hitherto withheld from the public.

A good many of them may even be quite unaware of the trend they have initiated. But with or without their knowledge, a new unifying symbol seems to be asserting itself. It is by no means sufficiently developed as yet to have gained universal acceptance. In fact, global shrinkage which breeds familiarity has, in some instances, bred disillusionment and apathy among those who are no longer strangers.

Still, the realization that we are all surely in it together may—with a little help—eventually lead to the recognition that a symbiotic relationship does indeed exist between "out there" and "in here" and that the making of a better world and the making of better men and women goes hand in hand.

Zimmer's statement, cited earlier,[4] thus contains not just one lesson but two. The first is: "Change yourself, and you inhabit a renovated world" while the second is: Realize that the world is changing, and you will become a new person.

Evoking a vision vividly reminiscent of Pico's vision in the Garden, Jung says "Everything now depends on man: immense power is given into his hand, and the question is whether he can resist the will to use it, and can temper his will with the spirit of love and wisdom."[6]

Like Pico, Jung places us squarely in the center of things—the eye of God upon us—and charges us with assuming responsibility for ourselves and the future of the planet: a daunting task in Pico's time; an even more formidable task today and in the years to come. It amounts to nothing less than building a genuinely brave new world, beyond polarity and insularity; a world founded on reconciliation and sustained by solidarity—with the poor, whoever and wherever they may be; with those who suffer from neglect and discrimination at the hands of oppressors and with those who allow their own inner being to wither away and die.

"The discovery of the reality of the poor is the origin of solidarity," writes the Salvadoran Jesuit scholar Jon Sobrino. "This truth is a primal call to the human dimension within any person and a challenge based on the fact that each of us is socially a part of all humankind. It brings with it a demand for change and conversion, for persons to recover their true identity."[6]

REFERENCES

1. Joseph Campbell, *The Hero with a Thousand Faces*. (Cleveland: World, 1956), pp. 388-389.

2. Marshall McLuhan, *The Medium Is the Message*. (New York: McGraw-Hill, 1965), p. vii.

3. C. G. Jung, *Aion*. (Princeton, NJ: Princeton University Press, 1959), p. 87.

4. Cf. supra, Ch. 13.

5. C. G. Jung, *Answer to Job* in Collected Works, vol. xi. (Princeton, NJ: Princeton University Press, 1969), p. 459.

6. Jon Sobrino, *Bearing with One Another in Faith* in Jon Sobrino and Juan Hernandez Pico, *Theology of Christian Solidarity*, trans. Phillip Berryman. (Maryknoll, NY: Orbis Books, 1985), p. 8.

15
The Tempest Revisited

> *There will come an America which we cannot foretell, a new creation on the face of the earth, a world beyond us . . . It only wants the miracle, the new, soft, creative wind: which does not blow yet. Meawhile we can only stand and wait, knowing that what is, is not. And we can listen to the sad, weird utterance of this classic America, watch the transmutation from men into machines and ghosts, hear the last metallic sounds. Perhaps we can see as well glimpses of the mystic transubstantiation.[1]*

What is surely one of the clearest, most poetic and prophetic expressions of the American myth has been provided to us in Shakespeare's *The Tempest*, the story of Prospero—Duke of Milan, conjurer and solitary seeker—who withdraws from civilization to find new meaning on a new shore.

Historians and literary critics now tend to agree that the bare outlines of the plot are based on fact: the misfortune which befell the flagship of a resupply mission on its way from England to the colony at Jamestown in 1609. A tropical storm had scattered the fleet, separating the flagship from the remainder and carrying it all the way to the Bermudas, where it ran aground.

All aboard, including the new governor of the colony, an admiral and some 150 men, got safely ashore. Eventually—almost a whole year later—the castaways at last arrived in Virginia, in two small sailing vessels they had built to replace the wrecked flagship. The accounts of their stay on the islands reached England soon thereafter, enhancing the image of a strange, enchanted—or in Shakespeare's words—brave new world.

Whether or not he himself actually read these accounts, the new world theme, the Golden Age theme had long filled the air and the subsequent discovery of new continents and alien peoples; new plants and flowers; hitherto unknown birds and beasts created a beguiling mixture of irreducible fact and utter wonderment that proved quite irresistible to an imagination such as his. The play—his next-to-last—was written in what has been called "the 'Shakespearean moment,' the hour when the Renaissance begins to pass through the crucible of reaction." [2] It was inspired, as much as anything, by the wish to retrieve what had remained of the Renaissance spirit and to preserve the best of it for posterity. For the poet himself, it was a summation; something of a valedictory; an attempt at creating a new world with the aid of magic.

Perhaps as a reaction to the vastly expanded physical world of his time, Shakespeare chose to reduce his theater world in size. The primary cast of characters numbers just four: Prospero himself; his angelic daughter Miranda; the mercurial, androgynous spirit Ariel, the symbol of Prospero's encapsulated creative powers, and savage Caliban, the anagrammatic cannibal, the old Adam.

The island serves as the alchemical vessel in which conflict and tension is resolved and a union of opposites is reached. In much the same way that Jung's psychology is prospective, Shakespeare's play is a prospective play: a parable of a future America; Prospero's vision of an American Dream.

Like Prospero, we may recall, the early colonizers gave up their place in civilized society for various reasons of their own, crossing the oceans in search of an ideal environment, an enclave where they might "work out the controlled magic of personal integration." [3]

Like them, Prospero shapes a new world in his own image and is shaped, molded and transformed by it in turn. He lets his spirit, Ariel, soar and weaves his magic spells and charms, using the island as a laboratory of the future and the other players like puppets on a string—but in the end, the marks he leaves on them and the pastoral environment are outweighed by the personal insights he gains. The *magnum opus* teaches the old magus that he himself was its subject all along.

When the time comes to bring it to a close, he knows what he must do: he must step down from his high perch and make peace with the erstwhile ruler of the island universe. Drowning his book of magic and breaking his magic wand, he takes a last look at his new world and the dark, primitive Caliban side of it and acknowledges the monster as part of himself.[4]

If his twelve years away from civilization have taught him nothing else, this alone is a singular accomplishment: the reconciliation between ego and shadow, as Jung would say; between master and slave; paleface and redskin; white man and black man, predating the Great Emancipator by more than two hundred years.

But if Prospero's march through the five acts of the play from Milan and back is to be read as a Shakespearean variant of the individuation process, one is left to wonder why he chooses to abandon the new world and indeed to ponder what will become of it once he and all the nobles and able-bodied seamen have sailed away.

Will the island be a better place now that the white men have granted it full independence or will it simply revert to the *status quo ante*? Will Caliban forget what the visitors from another world have told him, taught him and done to him or will he have acquired wisdom and culture? Is there a way for Caliban and Ariel to reconcile their differences and form a more perfect union of free spirits?

Many or all of these questions remain unanswered as Prospero rings down the curtain and asks for our indulgence and applause. He tells us that *The Tempest* is a theater piece—no more and certainly no less. Its theater is a *theatrum mundi*; its history is a history of the world and of Prospero's magic microcosm; its politics and power struggles are those of mortal men—and the tempest itself is the storm which rages without and within.

Like Jung, Shakespeare leaves us with an eidetic image. He has taken us this far. He has shown us and taught us how to conduct such an experiment and now seems to be saying: I am putting the pieces back where they were and leaving it to posterity to try its hand at solving this puzzle. Caliban rules the world below, Ariel rules the world above—place yourself in the middle and hold the balance between them.

The props have been removed; the players and musicians have gone home or perhaps only to the nearest pub. The stage is bare once again; but we know—as Shakespeare has known all along—that the island never really was uninhabited; that there is no such thing as an empty world, new or old, and that in order to win any world which is to serve as a common habitat for man and beast and friend and foe we must recapture that magnificent, enchanted, early moment of our existence when magicians were still in control; when a peaceable (if somewhat grudging) relationship between nature and spirit was still possible; when **the opposites** still lived in harmony and creative tension.

REFERENCES

1. D. H. Lawrence, *The Symbolic Meaning*. (New York: Viking, 1964), pp. 29-31.

2. Frances A. Yates, *The Occult Philosophy in the Elizabethan Age*. (London: Routledge & Kegan Paul, 1979), p. 163.

3. G. Wilson Knight, *The Crown of Life*. (New York: Barnes & Noble, 1966), p. 255.

4. William Shakespeare, *The Tempest* [Arden Edition]. (London: Methuen, 1958), p. 130.

BIBLIOGRAPHY

Rather than present the reader with an extended list of sources, I have prepared a brief and somewhat eclectic selection of materials which I have found helpful in dealing with the subject matter at hand and which, to my mind, most aptly reflect the mood I was trying to express in these pages.

Many of the titles are readily available as reprints and paperbacks; but some may only be obtainable at larger public libraries or at colleges and universities.

If familiar, they may bear reexamination. If not, they may provide new insights and points of departure for further exploration and discovery.

1. East-West Relations

Barghoorn, Frederick C., and Thomas F. Remington, *Politics in the USSR*. Boston, Toronto: Little, Brown & Co., 1986.

Bialer, Seweryn, *The Soviet Paradox: External Expansion, Internal Decline*. New York: Knopf, 1986.

Cohen, Stephen F., Alexander Rabinowitch, and Robert Sharlet, eds., *The Soviet Union Since Stalin*. Bloomington: Indiana State University Press, 1980.

Gong, Gerrit W., Angela E. Stent, and Rebecca V. Strode, *Areas of Challenge for Soviet Foreign Policy in the 1980s*. Bloomington: Indiana University Press, 1984.

Sakharov, Andrei, *Progress, Coexistence and Intellectual Freedom*. New York: Norton, 1968.

2. Future

Balasuriya, Tissa, *Planetary Theology*. Maryknoll, NY: Orbis Books, 1984.

Capra, Fritjof, and Charlene Spretnak, *Green Politics: The Global Promise*. New York: E. P. Dutton, 1984.

Fromm, Erich, *To Have or to Be*. New York: Bantam Books, 1981.

Griffiths, John, *Three Tomorrows: American, British and Soviet Science Fiction*. Totowa, NJ: Barnes & Noble, 1980.

Hillegas, Mark R., *The Future as Nightmare: H. G. Wells and the Anti-Utopians*. London: Oxford University Press, 1967.

Hughes, Barry B., *World Futures: A Critical Analysis of Alternatives*. Baltimore: Johns Hopkins University Press, 1985.

Manuel, Frank E., ed., *Utopias and Utopian Thought*. Boston: Beacon Press, 1967.

Osiatynski, Wiktor, *Contrasts: Soviet and American Thinkers Discuss the Future*. New York: MacMillan, 1984.

3. Jungian Psychology

Bryant, Christopher, *Jung and the Christian Way*. Minneapolis: Seabury Press, 1983.

Harding, M. Esther, *The 'I' and the 'Not-I': A Study in the Development of Consciousness*. Princeton, NJ: Princeton University Press, 1973.

Hillman, James, *Insearch: Psychology and Religion*. Dallas: Spring, 1978.

Inter Views: Conversations with Laura Pozzo. New York: Harper & Row, 1983.

Jaffé, Aniela, *The Myth of Meaning*. Zurich: Daimon, 1984.

Jung, Carl Gustav, *The Collected Works*, Vols. 1-20. Edited by Gerhard Adler, Michael Fordham and Herbert Read. Translated by R. F. C. Hull. (Bollingen Series XX.) New York: Pantheon Books and Princeton, NJ: Princeton Univeristy Press, 1953ff.

———*Memories, Dreams, Reflections*. Translated by Richard and Clara Winston. New York: Pantheon Books, 1962.

Samuels, Andrew, *Jung and the Post-Jungians*. London, Boston: Routledge & Kegan Paul, 1985.

Sanford, John A., *The Man Who Wrestled with God: Light from the Old Testament on the Psychology of Individuation*. New York: Paulist Press, 1981.

Ulanov, Ann B., *Receiving Woman: Studies in the Psychology and Theology of the Feminine*. Philadelphia: Westminster Press, 1981.

4. Religion and Liberation Theology

Brown, Robert McAfee, *Theology in a New Key*. Philadelphia: Westminster Press, 1978.

Liebman, Robert C., and Robert Wuthnow, *The New Christian Right*. New York: Aldine Publishing Co., 1983.

McLoughlin, William G., *Revivals, Awakenings and Reform*. Chicago: University of Chicago Press, 1978.

Mahan, Brian, and Dale L. Richesin, eds., *The Challenge of Liberation Theology: A First World Response*. Maryknoll, NY: Orbis Books, 1981.

Niebuhr, H. Richard, *The Kingdom of God in America*. New York: Harper Bros., 1937.

Quebedeaux, Richard, *By What Authority: The Rise of Personality Cults in American Christianity*. San Francisco: Harper & Row, 1982.

Rifkin, Jeremy, and Ted Howard, *The Emerging Order: God in an Age of Scarcity*. New York: G. P. Putnam's Sons, 1979.

Soelle, Dorothee (with Shirley Cloyes), *To Work and To Love: A Theology of Creation*. Philadelphia: Fortress Press, 1984.

Witvliet, Theo, *A Place in the Sun: An Introduction to Liberation Theology in the Third World*. Translated by John Bowden. Maryknoll, NY: Orbis Books, 1985.

5. Renaissance

Cassirer, Ernst, *The Individual and the Cosmos in Renaissance Philosophy*. Translated by Mario Domandi. Oxford: Blackwell, 1962.

Giamatti, A. Bartlett, *The Earthly Paradise and the Renaissance Epic*. Princeton, NJ: Princeton University Press, 1966.

Kristeller, Paul O., *Renaissance Thought and Its Sources*. New York: Columbia University Press, 1979.

Mazzeo, J. Anthony, *Renaissance and Revolution*. New York: Pantheon Books, 1965.

Robb, N. A., *Neoplatonism of the Italian Renaissance*. London: Allen & Unwin, 1935.

Wind, Edgar, *Pagan Mysteries of the Renaissance*. New York: Barnes & Noble, 1968.

6. Science

Aleksander, Igor and Piers Burnett, *The Robot Becomes Reality: Reinventing Man*. New York: Holt, Rinehart & Winston, 1983.

Bohr, Niels, *Essays 1958-1962 on Atomic Physics and Human Knowledge*. New York, London: Interscience Publishers, 1963.

Briggs, John P. and David F. Peat, *The Emerging Science of Wholeness*. New York: Simon & Schuster, 1984.

Davies, Paul, *God and the New Physics*. New York: Simon & Schuster, 1983.

Fraser, Julius T., ed., *The Voices of Time*. Amherst, MA: University of Massachusetts Press, 1981.

Heisenberg, Werner, *Physics and Beyond*. New York: Harper & Row, 1971.

Jantsch, Erich and Conrad H. Waddington, *Evolution and Consciousness*. Reading, MA: Addison-Wesley, 1976.

Roszak, Theodore, *The Cult of Information*. New York: Pantheon, 1986.

Simons, Geoff, *Are Computers Alive?*. Boston: Birkhäuser, 1983.

Weizenbaum, Joseph, *Computer Power and Human Reason*. New York: W. H. Freeman & Co., 1976.

Wilber, Ken, *Quantum Questions*. Boulder, CO, London: Shambhala, 1984.

7. Shakespeare

Armstrong, John, *The Paradise Myth*. London: Oxford University Press, 1969.

Fiedler, Leslie A., *The Stranger in Shakespeare*. New York: Stein & Day, 1972.

Frye, Northrop, *Northrop Frye on Shakespeare*. New Haven, London: Yale University Press, 1986.

Kermode, Frank, *William Shakespeare: The Final Plays*. London: Longmans Green, 1963.

Knight, G. Wilson, *The Crown of Life*. New York: Barnes & Noble, 1966.

Yates, Frances, *The Rosicrucian Enlightenment*. London: Routledge & Kegan Paul, 1972.

8. Third Reich

Abel, Theodore F., *The Nazi Movement: Why Hitler Came to Power*. New York: Atherton Press, 1966.

Allen, William S., *The Nazi Seizure of Power: The Experience of a Single German Town*. Chicago: Quadrangle Books, 1965.

Binion, Rudolf, *Hitler Among the Germans*. Oxford, New York, Amsterdam: Elsevier, 1976.

Bracher, Karl Dietrich, *The German Dictatorship*. New York, Washington: Praeger, 1970.

Cantril, Hadley, *The Psychology of Social Movements*. New York: Wiley, 1941.

Cohn, Norman, *Warrant for Genocide*. New York: Harper & Row, 1966.

Gallin, Mary Alice, *Ethical and Religious Factors of the German Resistance to Hitler*. Washington, DC: Catholic University Press, 1955.

Mitscherlich, Alexander and Margarete, *The Inability to Mourn*. New York: Grove Press, 1975.

Maier, Charles S., Stanley Hoffmann, and Andrew Gould, eds., *The Rise of the Nazi Regime: Historical Reassessments*. Boulder, CO, London: Westview Press, 1986.

Neumann, Sigmund, *Permanent Revolution*. New York: Praeger, 1965.

Rubenstein, Richard L., *The Age of Triage*. Boston: Beacon Press, 1983.

Wheeler-Bennett, John, *The Nemesis of Power: The German Army in Politics 1918-1945*. New York: Viking Press, 1967.

9. U. S. History and Civilization

Adams, Henry, *The Education of Henry Adams*. Boston: Houghton Mifflin, 1973.

Becker, Carl L., *How New Will the Better World Be?* New York: Knopf, 1944.

Boorstin, Daniel J., *Image: A Guide to Pseudo-Events in America*. New York: Atheneum, 1962.

Cater, Douglas and Richard Adler, eds., *Television as a Social Force*. New York: Praeger, 1975.

Halttunen, Karen, *Confidence Men and Painted Women*. New Haven, London: Yale University Press, 1982.

Lewis, R. W. B., *American Adam: Innocence, Tragedy and Tradition in the Nineteenth Century*. Chicago: University of Chicago Press, 1955.

McNeill, William H., *The Great Frontier: Freedom and Hierarchy in Modern Times*. Princeton, NJ: Princeton University Press, 1983.

Marx, Leo, *The Machine in the Garden: Technology and the Pastoral Ideal in America*. London, Oxford, New York: Oxford University Press, 1964.

Miller, Perry, *Errand into the Wilderness*. New York: Harper & Row, 1964.

O'Gorman, Edmundo, *The Invention of America*. Westport, CN: Greenwood Press, 1977.

Sanford, Charles L., *Quest for Paradise: Europe and the American Moral Imagination*. Urbana, IL: University of Illinois Press, 1961.

Slotkin, Richard, *Regeneration Through Violence: The Mythology of the American Frontier 1600-1850*. Middletown, CN: Wesleyan University Press, 1973.

Tinder, Glenn E., *Political Thinking: The Perennial Questions*. Boston: Little, Brown & Co., 1979.

Yoder, R. A., *Emerson and the Orphic Poet in America*. Berkeley: University of California Press, 1978.

10. Weimar Republic

Bessel, Richard and E. J. Feuchtwanger, eds., *Social Change and Political Development in Weimar Germany*. Totowa, NJ: Barnes & Noble, 1981.

Fussell, Paul, *The Great War and Modern Memory*. New York, London: Oxford University Press, 1975.

Kracauer, Siegfried, *From Caligari to Hitler: A Psychological History of the German Film*. Princeton, NJ: Princeton University Press, 1947.

Stern, Fritz, *The Politics of Cultural Despair: A Study in the Rise of the Germanic Ideology*. Berkeley: University of California Press, 1961.

von Klemperer, Klemens, *Germany's New Conservatism*. Princeton, NJ: Princeton University Press, 1957.

Waite, Robert G. L., *Vanguard of Nazism: The Free Corps Movement in Postwar Germany 1918-1923*. New York: Norton, 1969.

INDEX

Adler, Alfred, 70
Alchemists, alchemy, 8, 9, 56, 66, 75, 86, 96
Allen, William, S., 36
American dream, xii, 16, 41-42, 96
Anima/animus, 85
Archetypes, 55, 81, 82, 83, 84, 86; *See also* anima/animus: ego: self: shadow
Arendt, Hannah, xi-xii

Barrett, William, 38
Beradt, Charlotte, 36
Bleibtreu, John, 80
Boff, Leonardo, 72, 77
Bok, Sissela, 24
Brown, Robert M., 59
Brownson, Orestes, 60
Burden, Hamilton T., 35

Caliban, 83, 96, 97, 98
Cameron, Kenneth W., 60

Campbell, Joseph, 89
Capitalism, capitalists, 56, 63, 64
Capra, Fritjof, 60, 66
Cassirer, Ernst, 8, 66-67
Civil War, 45, 46
Cohen, Stephen F., 65
Cole, Thomas, 43
Collectivism, 12, 76
Communism, communists, 34, 56, 63, 64
Consciousness, 9, 73, 76, 81, 83, 86
Conservatism, conservatives, 14, 32, 52
Convergence, 8, 65, 66
Coolidge, Louis A., 45
Cooper, James Fenimore, 42, 43
Crawley, Alfred E., 1
Curti, Merle, 44, 45

Dewey, George, [Adm.], 45
Dreams, 73, 86; Jung's 1909 dream of cellar and cave, 80-81; of

Germans under Hitler, 36; of paradise, 6, 41; of two magicians, 1-4, 58

Edwards, Jonathan, 41
Ego, 72, 73, 84, 86, 87, 97
Eliade, Mircea, 6, 9
Emancipation, 50, 58, 59, 86, 87
Emerson, Ralph Waldo, 58, 87
Evil, xi, 35, 45

Fear, 36, 56, 58; freedom from, 57, 59, 66
Ferlinghetti, Lawrence, 38
Four Freedoms, 57-58
Freud, Sigmund, 70, 80
Frey-Rohn, Liliane, 70

Gay, Peter, 13
Gaylin, Willard, 15-16
God, 8, 49, 55, 74, 76; and sacrilege [Kennan], 57, and "spiritual circuit" [Panofsky], 68; and self, 73, 74, 85; as consumer commodity, 50
Gorbachev, Mikhail, ix
Goswami, Amit, 66
Graham, Billy, 14

Harding, M. Esther, 72
Herf, Jeffrey, 22
Hillman, James, 39, 40
Hindenburg, Paul von: elected German president in 1925, 22-23; involved in scandal, 23-24; reelected to presidency in 1932, 27-28; swears in Hitler as chancellor, 32
Hitler, Adolf, xi, 3, 13, 15, 16, 19, 29, 30, 34-35, 39; as media personality, 34; as 1932 presidential candidate, 28; as savior, 29; as warlord, 19; Jung's assessment of, 34; legacy of, 15; sworn in as chancellor, 32

Hofstadter, Richard, 44
Holocaust, 32, 84
Homer, 8
Human dignity, 7, 10, 19, 78
Humanism, humanists, 8, 9, 33, 60, 75, 91

Individual, ix, xi, xii, 10, 18, 67, 75
Individualism, 75, 76, 78
Individuation, individuation process, 72, 73, 82, 85, 86, 89, 97; defined by Jung, xii, 72, 76, 81; and individualism compared, 75

Jung, Carl Gustav, ix, x, xi, xii-xiii, 1, 2, 16, 66, 70, 77, 90, 93, 96, 98; and individuation process, xii, 72, 76, 81, 89; and self, 73, 74, 87; assessment of Hitler, 34; on alchemy, 9; on anima/animus, 85; on conjunction of opposites, 86, 92; on dream of two magicians, 2; on "metamorphosis of gods," 77; on own dream of cellar and cave, 81; on religious experience, 74, 75; on shadow, 83-84; on UFOs, 54-55; on "unitary world," 78; on "unity of mankind," 62; on "unus mundus," 68

Kennan, George F., 57
Kennedy, Moorhead, 65
Khomeini, Ruhollah (Ayatollah), ix
Knight, G. Wilson, 97
Knight-Patterson, W. M., 24
Koestler, Arthur, 30
Kohn, Hans, 27
Kracauer, Siegfried, 28-29

Laqueur, Walter, 18
Lawrence, D. H., 95

Lenin, V. I., 18
Lepsius, M. Rainer, 32
Lerner, Max, 10
Liberals, 12, 14, 23, 27, 30, 33, 56
Liberation theology: and *aggiornamento*, 77; and emancipation of the masses, 50; and love [Brown], 59; and solidarity with the poor [Sobrino], 93;
Lincoln, Abraham, 46, 97

Machiavelli, Niccolò, 10
Magic, magus, xii, 1, 3, 8, 9, 96, 97
Mannheim, Karl, 25
McLoughlin, William G., 52-53
McLuhan, Marshall, 90
Mead, Margaret, 54
Media, 31, 33; used by Hitler, 34; used by U. S. fundamentalists, 49-51
Medvedev, Zhores, 64
Military power, x, xii, 20, 34; and moral responsibility, xii, 57; and weapons arsenals, 57; in Spanish-American War, 44-45; used by Hitler, 19
Mythology, myths, 3, 7, 54, 56, 73, 82, 84, 86

National Socialism, 13, 21, 29, 30, 33-34, 36; and conformism, 35; reassessment of, 16
Nietzsche, Friedrich, 38-39
Nihilism, 13, 38-39; revolution of [Rauschning], 15
Noble, Louis L., 43
Nonbelievers, 4, 35, 76, 78
Novak, Michael, 48
Nuclear age, 54, 65, 84

Opposites: conjunction of, 2, 46, 64, 68, 73, 86, 96; problem of, 92
Osiatynski, Wiktor, 62

Panofsky, Erwin, 68
Paradise, 6, 7, 41, 55; as "state of unity" [Eliade], 6; in theology student's dream, 2-3
Payne Robert, 32
Phillips, Kevin P., 52
Picard, Max, 13, 14
Pico della Mirandola, Giovanni, 9, 67, 75, 93; as "Prince of Concord," xi, 10; "Oration on the Dignity of Man," 7-8
Pound, Ezra, 20
Projection, 39, 63
Prospero, xii, 83, 95, 96, 97, 98

Quebedeaux, Richard, 49, 50, 51

Rauschning, Hermann, 15
Reagan, Ronald, ix
Religion, 3, 75; in America, 42, 48-49; need for, 29, 74
Renaissance, x, xi, xii, 6-9, 66; and quest for harmony, 9; and "Shakespearean moment" [Yates], 96; as response to waning culture, 6; end of, 9
Riencourt, Amaury de, 42
Roosevelt, Franklin D., 57, 66
Roosevelt, Theodore, 44-45
Rotondi, Pasquale, 6

Sanford, Charles L., 41
Sartre, Jean-Paul, 14
Science fiction, 54-56
Self, 73, 74, 84, 85, 87; as midpoint, 87; as new center, 72; as "psychic wholeness" [Jung], 74
Shadow, 16, 82, 85, 97; as *Doppelgänger*, 82; as moral problem, 83; confrontation with [Jung], 83-84
Shakespeare, William, xii, 95-98

Singer, June, 82
Sobrino, Jon, 93
Soul, xi, xii, 56, 87; "finished soul" [Emerson], 58; immortality of, 76; loss of, 40, 42; of America, 40, 42
Soviet, Soviet Union, 62, 64, 65
Spanish-American War, 44-45
Spretnak, Charlene, 60
Stoner, John, 36

"The Tempest," xii, 95-98
Tocqueville, Alexis de, 48, 49
Totalitarianism, xi, 12, 13, 16, 30, 64; as political religion, 3, 29
Traditional politics, 56, 91; in United States and Soviet Union, 63; in Weimar Republic, 12, 14, 24-25, 28, 30
Transcendentalism, 60
Turner, Frederick Jackson, 44

UFOs, 54-55
Unconscious, 76, 81, 86
Unitary World, xii, 66, 68
United States: as big power, x-xii; as myth, 95; as New Eden, 41; and Civil War, 45-46; and extremism, 16, 51-52; caught in dilemma, x-xi; closing of frontier, 44; lost innocence of, 43; new awakening in, 52-53; new political framework for, 60; religion in, 48-49; soul of, 40, 42; Spanish-American War, 44-45; television evangelists in, x, 49-51
Unity, 6, 9; and new physics, 67-68; of mankind [Jung], 62

Voegelin, Eric, 12, 29

Weimar Republic, 12, 14, 15, 22-26; and gerontocracy, 25; and Nazi rise to power, 29-31; as ungovernable system, 14; 1925 presidential election, 22-23; 1932 presidential election, 28
Wheeler, John, 67
Wilber, Ken, 66
World War I, 18-21, 23

Yates, Dame Frances, 96
Young and old, 89-92

Zimmer, Heinrich, 85, 92